The
English Springer Spaniel

An Owner's Guide To

A HAPPY HEALTHY PET

Howell Book House

Howell Book House
A Simon & Schuster Macmillan Company
1633 Broadway
New York, NY 10019

Library of Congress Cataloging-in-Publication Data
Callahan, Carol (Carol R.)
The English Springer spaniel : an owner's guide to a happy healthy pet/Carol Callahan.
   p. cm.
   Includes bibliographical references.
   ISBN 0-87605-482-3
1. English springer spaniels. I. Title.
SF429.E7C34 1996
636.7'52—dc20   96-20449
            CIP

Manufactured in the United States of America
10 9 8 7 6 5 4 3

Series Director: Dominique De Vito
Series Assistant Director: Ariel Cannon
Book Design: Michele Laseau
Cover Design: Iris Jeromnimon
Illustration: Jeff Yesh
Photography:
   Front cover photos by Paulette Braun/Pets by Paulette
   Back cover photograph by Judith Strom
Joan Balzarini: 96
Mary Bloom: 96, 136, 145
Paulette Braun/Pets by Paulette: 13, 32, 33, 59, 74, 81, 96
Buckinghamhill American Cocker Spaniels: 148
Courtesy of the American Kennel Club: 18, 19
Courtesy of Carol Callahan: 5, 40
Sean Cox: 134
Dr. Ian Dunbar: 98, 101, 116–117, 122, 123, 127
Ellice Hauta: 28
Dan Lyons: 96
Cathy Merrithew: 129
Scott McKiernan/Zuma: 9, 25, 30, 65
Liz Palika: 133
Cheryl Primeau: 51, 53
Susan Rezy: 96–97
Judith Strom: 2–3, 7, 12, 21, 26, 27, 31, 38–39, 42, 44, 47, 56, 68, 96, 107, 110, 128, 130, 135, 137, 139, 140, 144, 149, 150
Jean Wentworth: 49, 62, 78
Kerrin Winter & Dale Churchill: 6, 48, 60, 61, 64

Contents

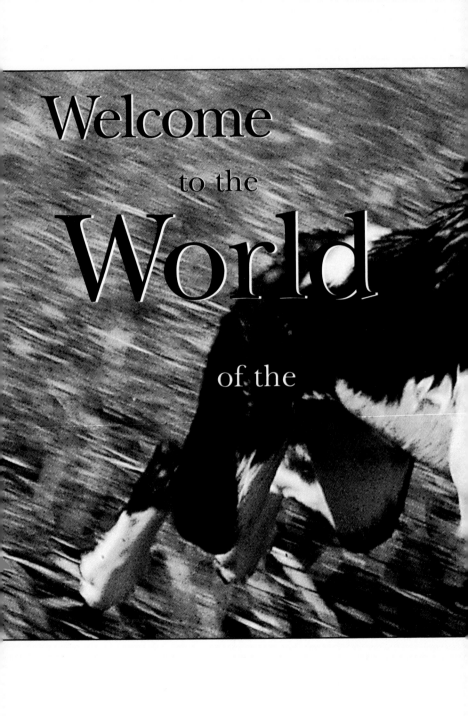

Welcome

to the

World

of the

part one

English Springer Spaniel

External Features of the English Springer Spaniel

Skull

Stop

Muzzle

Crest

Neck

Withers

Shoulder

Back

Stifle or Knee

Toes

Hock

chapter 1

What
Is an
English Springer
Spaniel?

One look at the English Springer Spaniel and you know why this is such a well-loved dog: He combines beauty, size and personality.

Look at his coat. It's soft and feathery in spots, but not too long. He is a striking pairing of black and white or brown and white, with big patches, little patches, even spotty patches.

Look at his face. Those adoring brown eyes, saying they'll love you no matter what. That nicely defined muzzle, not too big, not too small,

just the right size for nudging at your hands for an extra pat. And those long, soft ears that blow in the wind as he runs drape around his face to give him that sweet expression.

Look at his athletic build: strong feet; solid legs; square, compact body. Not too tall, not too short—a perfect size for the sometimes fit/sometimes flabby family, content to exercise well and lounge well.

Look at how he acts. Devoted to his human family. Mild-mannered. Good-natured. A go-anywhere, do-anything kind of dog who always seems to be smiling at you. This is the English Springer Spaniel.

Taking a Closer Look

All pure-bred dogs were developed for particular reasons (more on history in Chapter 2). Suffice it to say that each breed is supposed to look a certain way and be instantly recognizable as that breed.

To keep breeding true, dog breeders developed "blueprints" of their breeds—standards by which they mea-

sured the success of their breeding programs. Each pure breed of dog has a standard, which describes in detail what the ideal specimen of that dog should look like. No "perfect" dog of any breed has been or will ever be bred, there are just those that come as close as possible (or not).

The breed standard is also what dog show judges use to evaluate the dogs in the show ring. The judges go over the dogs in the ring and keep mental notes of which parts are closest—and furthest—from the standard.

Studying your breed's standard is a good way to learn about what generations of English Springer Spaniel breeders have been striving to produce. The standard is written by the breed's parent club, the English Springer Spaniel Field Trial Association, and it was most recently reformatted and approved by the American Kennel Club in 1989.

Below is the Official Standard for the English Springer Spaniel. To help you understand each point, I have provided some commentary after the official wording. The Official Standard is in regular type, the commentary is in italics. Read carefully while looking at your wonderful pet. How does your dog compare to the standard?

Official Standard for the English Springer Spaniel

GENERAL APPEARANCE

The English Springer Spaniel is a medium-sized sporting dog, with a compact body and a docked tail. His coat is moderately long, with feathering on his legs, ears, chest and brisket. His pendulous ears, soft gentle expression, sturdy build and friendly wagging tail proclaim him unmistakably a member of the ancient family of Spaniels. He is above all a well-proportioned dog, free from exaggeration, nicely balanced in every part. His carriage is proud and upstanding, body deep, legs strong and muscular, with enough length to carry him with ease.

This show dog has his ears wrapped so they don't get dirty before he goes into the ring.

Taken as a whole, the English Springer Spaniel suggests power, endurance and agility. He looks the part of a dog that can go, and keep going, under difficult hunting conditions. At his best, he is endowed with style, symmetry, balance and enthusiasm and is every inch a sporting dog of distinct spaniel character, combining beauty and utility.

What comes across most about the Springer's general appearance is that he should look the part of the capable hunter that he is—"well proportioned . . . free from exaggeration, nicely balanced in every part." As you study his individual parts in more detail, keep this in mind. And don't forget that "soft gentle expression" and "friendly wagging tail"—so telling of the English Springer Spaniel. The Springer is built to do his day's work with style and gusto, and enjoy it.

SIZE, PROPORTION AND SUBSTANCE

The Springer is built to cover rough ground with agility and reasonable speed. His structure suggests the capacity for endurance. He is to be kept to medium size. Ideal height at the shoulder for dogs is 20 inches; for bitches, it is 19 inches. Those more than one inch under or over the breed ideal are to be faulted.

A 20-inch dog, well-proportioned and in good condition, will weight approximately 50 pounds; a 19-inch bitch will weigh approximately 40 pounds. The length of the body (measured from the point of shoulder to point of buttocks) is slightly greater than the height at the withers. The dog too long in body, especially when long in loin, tires easily and lacks the compact outline characteristic of the breed. A dog too short in body for the length of his legs, a condition which destroys balance and restricts gait, is equally undesirable. A Springer with correct substance appears well-knit and sturdy, with good bone; however, he is never coarse or ponderous.

> **WHAT IS A BREED STANDARD?**
>
> A breed standard—a detailed description of an individual breed—is meant to portray the *ideal* specimen of that breed. This includes ideal structure, temperament, gait, type—all aspects of the dog. Because the standard describes an ideal specimen, it isn't based on any particular dog. It is a concept against which judges compare actual dogs and breeders strive to produce dogs. At a dog show, the dog that wins is the one that comes closest, in the judge's opinion, to the standard for its breed. Breed standards are written by the breed parent clubs, the national organizations formed to oversee the well-being of the breed. They are voted on and approved by the members of the parent clubs.

What's important to notice here is the emphasis on correct size. This is because a larger or smaller dog would have a build that caused it to work differently. A smaller dog would be like the Springer's close cousin the Cocker Spaniel, who has his own standard based on his job. A bigger dog would make the Springer less the compact, close-working hunter he's supposed to be. After the weighing and measuring are done, however, it is important for the dog to be balanced. Refer back to "general appearance" and keep reminding yourself that a well-built dog is balanced— "well-knit" and "sturdy . . . in no way coarse or ponderous."

HEAD

The head is impressive without being heavy. Its beauty lies in a combination of strength and refinement. It is important that its size and proportion be in balance with the rest of the dog. Viewed in profile, the head appears approximately the same length as the neck and blends with the body in substance. The stop, eyebrows and chiseling of the bony structure around the eye sockets contribute to the Springer's beautiful and characteristic expression, which is alert, kindly and trusting. The **eyes**, more than any other feature, are the essence of the Springer's appeal. Correct size, shape, placement and color influence expression and attractiveness. The eyes are of medium size and oval in shape, set rather well-apart and fairly deep in their sockets. The color of the iris harmonizes with the color of the coat, preferably dark hazel in the liver and white dogs and black or deep brown in the black and white dogs. Eye rims are fully pigmented and match the coat in color. Lids are tight with little or no haw showing. Eyes that are small, round or protruding, as well as eyes that are yellow or brassy in color, are highly undesirable. **Ears** are long and fairly wide, hanging close to the cheeks with no tendency to stand up or out. The ear leather is thin and approximately long enough to reach the tip of the nose. Correct ear set is on a level with the eye and not too far back on the skull. The **skull** is medium-length and fairly broad, flat on top and slightly rounded at the sides and back. The occiput bone is inconspicuous. As the skull rises from the foreface, it makes a stop, divided by a groove, or

This is "Robert," the 1993 Westminster Best in Show winner, with his handler, Mark Threlfall. Compare his build and appearance with what you read here.

fluting, between the eyes. The groove disappears as it reaches the middle of the forehead. The amount of stop is moderate. It must not be a pronounced feature; rather it is a subtle rise where the muzzle joins the upper head. It is emphasized by the groove and by the position and shape of the eyebrows, which are well-developed. The **muzzle** is approximately the same length as the skull and one-half the width of the skull. Viewed in profile, the toplines of the skull and muzzle lie in approximately parallel planes. The nasal bone is straight, with no inclination downward toward the tip of the nose, the latter giving an undesirable downfaced look. Neither is the nasal bone concave, resulting in a "dish-faced" profile; nor convex, giving the dog a Roman nose. The cheeks are flat, and the face is well-chiseled under the eyes. **Jaws** are of sufficient length to allow the dog to carry game easily: fairly square, lean and strong. The upper lips come down full and rather square to cover the line of the lower jaw, however, the lips are never pendulous or exaggerated. The nose is fully-pigmented, liver or black in color, depending on the color of the coat. The nostrils are well-opened and broad. Teeth are strong, clean, of good size and ideally meet in a close scissors bite. An even bite or one or two incisors slightly out of line are minor faults. Undershot, overshot and wry jaws are serious faults and are to be severely penalized.

Why, you may ask, is the description of the Springer's head so long? Because it is the source of some very important

THE AMERICAN KENNEL CLUB

Familiarly referred to as "the AKC," the American Kennel Club is a nonprofit organization devoted to the advancement of pure-bred dogs. The AKC maintains a registry of recognized breeds and adopts and enforces rules for dog events including shows, obedience trials, field trials, hunting tests, lure coursing, herding, earthdog trials, agility and the Canine Good Citizen program. It is a club of clubs, established in 1884 and composed, today, of over 500 autonomous dog clubs throughout the United States. Each club is represented by a delegate; the delegates make up the legislative body of the AKC, voting on rules and electing directors. The American Kennel Club maintains the Stud Book, the record of every dog ever registered with the AKC, and publishes a variety of materials on purebred dogs, including a monthly magazine, books and numerous educational pamphlets. For more information, contact the AKC at the address listed in Chapter 13, "Resources," and look for the names of their publications in Chapter 12, "Recommended Reading."

functions— smell, vision, jaw power and expression, to name a few. Variations in size of muzzle affect scenting ability by changing the amount of air traveling through and reaching the membranes containing scent glands. The shape of the mouth and jaw are designed so that the Springer can retrieve landfowl without pressure or strain. The size, shape and color of the eyes are all crucial to giving the correct expression to the Springer—the expression that's won the heart of anyone he meets.

NECK, TOPLINE, BODY

The **neck** is moderately long, muscular, clean and slightly arched at the crest. It blends gradually and smoothly into sloping shoulders. The portion of the topline from withers to tail is firm and slopes very gently. The **body** is short-coupled, strong and compact. The **chest** is deep, reaching the level of the elbows, with well-developed forechest; however, it is not so wide or round as to interfere with the action of the front legs. **Ribs** are fairly long, springing gradually to the middle of the body, then tapering as they approach the end of the ribbed section. The underline stays level with the elbows to a slight upcurve at the flank. The **back** is straight, strong and essentially level. **Loins** are strong, short and slightly arched. **Hips** are nicely-rounded, blending smoothly into the hind legs. The croup slopes gently to the set of the tail, and tail-set follows the natural line of the croup. The **tail** is carried horizontally or slightly elevated and displays a characteristic lively, merry action, particularly when the dog is on game. A clamped tail (indicating timidity or undependable temperament) is to be faulted, as is a tail carried at a right angle to the backline in Terrier fashion.

Again, these physical characteristics are detailed so breeders can keep the dog looking the way he needs to in order to do his job and be instantly recognizable as the English Springer Spaniel and no other spaniel. With so many close cousins, these details are necessary to the success of a breeding program.

FOREQUARTERS

Efficient movement in front calls for proper forequarter assembly. The **shoulder blades** are flat, fairly close together at the tips, molding smoothly into the contour of the body. Ideally, when measured from the top of the withers to the point of the shoulder to the elbow, the shoulder blade and upper arm are of apparent equal length, forming an angle of nearly 90 degrees; this sets the front legs well under the body and places the elbows directly beneath the tips of the shoulder blades. **Elbows** lie close to the body. **Forelegs** are straight with the same degree of size continuing to the foot. Bone is strong, slightly flattened, not too round or too heavy. **Pasterns** are short, strong and slightly sloping, with no suggestion of weakness. **Dewclaws** are usually removed. **Feet** are round or slightly oval. They are compact and well-arched, of medium size, with thick pads, and well-feathered between the toes.

Proper hind-quarters are what give this dog his ability to push off from shore and dive in after downed game.

HINDQUARTERS

The Springer should be worked and shown in hard, muscular condition with well-developed hips and thighs. His whole rear assembly suggests strength and driving power. Thighs are broad and muscular. Stifle joints are strong. For functional efficiency, the angulation of the hindquarter is never greater than that of the forequarter, and not appreciably less. The hock joints are somewhat rounded, not small and sharp in contour. Rear pasterns are short (about one-third the distance from the hip joints to the foot) and strong, with good bone. When viewed from behind, the rear pasterns are parallel. Dewclaws are usually removed. The feet are the same as in front, except that they are smaller and often more compact.

This is a classic liver-and-white Springer. Notice the thicker fur around his ears and chest.

A dog with a beautiful head, perfect back and sufficient rib cage is still nothing without good legs and feet. After all, these are what propel and carry him through the field. They take most of the beating for him. A structural flaw in the legs or feet could incapacitate a hunting dog forever. If he doesn't have the correct bone size and position, he won't move right. If he doesn't move right, he'll tire more easily or will be less inclined to do his job. If his feet are thin or narrow, they won't help him trudge through rough terrain or get traction in the mud.

Look at any athlete who needs to propel himself forward in a sport. He needs strong thighs and knees, and he needs the skeleton to support them.

13

COAT

The Springer has an outer coat and an undercoat.
On the body, the outer coat is of medium length, flat
or wavy and is easily distinguishable from the undercoat, which is short, soft and dense. The quantity of
undercoat is affected by climate and season. When in
combination, outer coat and undercoat serve to make
the dog substantially waterproof, weatherproof and
thornproof. On ears, chest, legs and belly the Springer
is nicely furnished with a fringe of feathering of moderate length and heaviness. On the head, front of the
forelegs, and below the hock joints on the front of the
hind legs, the hair is short and fine. The coat has
the clean, glossy, "live" appearance indicative of good
health. It is legitimate to trim about the head, ears,
neck and feet, to remove dead undercoat, and to thin
and shorten excess feathering as required to enhance
a smart, functional appearance. The tail may be
trimmed, or well-fringed with wavy feathering. Above
all, the appearance should be natural. Overtrimming,
especially of the body coat, or any chopped, barbered
or artificial effect is to be penalized in the show ring, as
is excessive feathering that destroys the clean outline
desirable in a sporting dog. Correct quality and condition of coat is to take precedence over quantity of coat.

*If your Springer's fur isn't naturally glossy and fine, with
more of it on his ears, chest, legs and belly, and if it isn't flat
or wavy, your dog won't look like a Springer. Beauty is in the
eye of the beholder, and if your dog's coat doesn't look like that
of the Springer at the dog show, you need not worry so long as
the coat meets the physical requirements of the breed. People
who show their dogs spend years learning grooming techniques to enhance their dogs' looks. You don't have to do that
to have a good-looking Springer, though keeping your dog
looking his best should be important to you.*

COLOR

All of the following combinations of colors and markings are equally acceptable: (1) Black or liver with
white markings or predominantly white with black or

liver markings; (2) Blue or liver roan; (3) Tricolor: black and white or liver and white with tan markings, usually found on eyebrows, cheeks, inside of ears and under the tail. Any white portion of the coat may be flecked with ticking. Off colors, such as lemon, red or orange, are not to place.

"Not to place" here refers to showing the dog. If your dog is any of the colors listed in the "to be penalized" phrase, a dog show judge will not place it (first, second, third or fourth) in the class. Most Springers are liver (brown) and white or black and white.

GAIT

The final test of the Springer's conformation and soundness is proper movement. Balance is the prerequisite to good movement. The front and rear assemblies must be equivalent in angulation and muscular development for the gait to be smooth and effortless. Shoulders which are well laid-back to permit a long stride are just as essential as the excellent rear quarters that provide driving power. Seen from the side, the Springer exhibits a long ground-covering stride and carries a firm back, with no tendency to dip, roach or roll from side to side. From the front, the legs swing forward in a free and easy manner. Elbows have free action from the shoulders, and the legs show no tendency to cross or interfere. From behind, the rear legs reach well under the body, following on a line with the forelegs. As speed increases, there is a natural tendency for the legs to converge toward a center line of travel. Movement faults include high-stepping, wasted motion, short, choppy stride, crabbing and moving with the feet wide, the latter giving roll or swing to the body.

If you read this section carefully and watch your dog in motion, you'll learn a lot about how a dog with a good build should move. It's interesting to compare what's written here with what you see your dog doing and what other Springers do. Remember, a standard describes an ideal dog, but it's important to know what you're looking for.

TEMPERAMENT

The typical Springer is friendly, eager to please, quick to learn and willing to obey. Such traits are conducive to tractability, which is essential for appropriate handler control in the field. In the show ring, he should exhibit poise and attentiveness and permit himself to be examined by the judge without resentment or cringing. Aggression toward people and aggression toward other dogs is not in keeping with sporting dog character and is not acceptable. Excessive timidity, with due allowance for puppies and novice exhibits, is to be equally penalized.

You can read more about how temperament is such an all-important characteristic of the English Springer Spaniel in Chapter 3, where we'll explore the world according to this breed.

SUMMARY

In evaluating the English Springer Spaniel, the overall picture is a primary consideration. One should look for *type*, which includes general appearance and outline, and also for *soundness*, which includes movement and temperament. Inasmuch as the dog with a smooth easy gait must be reasonably sound and well-balanced, he is to be highly regarded—however, not to the extent of forgiving him for not looking like an English Springer Spaniel. An atypical dog, too short or long in leg length or foreign in head or expression, may move well, but he is not to be preferred over a good all-round specimen that has a minor fault in movement. It must be remembered that the English Springer Spaniel is first and foremost a sporting dog of the Spaniel family, and he must *look, behave* and *move* in character.

Approved February 12, 1994

A Final Thought

This is a lot of information for someone new to this breed or to purebred dogs. Don't feel like you have to understand it all or that your dog must measure up to its "standard." Think of the standard as a description of the Springer written by people who've known and loved this breed for centuries. There's a lot of history here, and learning about your breed's standard is another way of getting to know him and his ancestors. The rest of the book will help, too.

chapter 2

The English Springer Spaniel's Ancestry

The English Springer is just one of many breeds of spaniel, a hunting dog whose land of origin is Spain. The breed is so well associated with the British Isles that it is hard to think of it working south of the English Channel, but indeed it did for many years—or at least its ancestors did. It took many more years of selective breeding to fix the type that we recognize today as the English Springer Spaniel.

About Spaniels

The first written account we have of the spaniel's use is in the *Livre de Chasse*. This 1387 text, penned by the French nobleman Gaston de

Foix, was reproduced as *The Master of Game* by Edward, the second Duke of York between 1406 and 1413. The book(s) described the spaniel as a good hound for hunting the hawk. They came from Spain, but were found in a number of countries.

Over 100 years later the British scholar Dr. John Caius wrote *Of Englishe Dogges* (1576), and said of the spaniel, "Of gentile dogges serving the hauke, and first of the Spaniell called in Latin Hispaniolus, there be two sorts: 1. The first findeth game on the land. 2. The other findeth game on the water."

The larger spaniel used to "spring" birds from their cover became known as the "springing" or Springer Spaniel. This is a 1938 champion, Ch. Rufton Roberto of Greenfair.

It is the land spaniel from whom our English Springer is descended. His job, according to Caius, was to "spryngeth the birde and betrayth flight by pursuite." Back then, hunters needed several types of dogs to bag their quarry. For example, if it was pheasant they were after—a bird who uses camouflage and flight to hide and escape from its enemies—the hunters would let their spaniels hunt the fields and flush out the birds. They would then send a hound dog or a hawk to chase and kill the bird and, possibly, a retriever to get and bring back the bird.

Land spaniels evolved into two types, too. There were the flushers, who worked as described here, and there were the "setters," who crouched down and snuck up on the bird, alerting the hunters to its location. The hunters would then throw a net over the area the dog was indicating, bagging the birds hiding there.

Another type of spaniel was the water spaniel, the variation that flushed like a land spaniel, but also retrieved downed game in the water.

WHERE DID DOGS COME FROM?

It can be argued that dogs were right there at man's side from the beginning of time. As soon as human beings began to document their own existence, the dog was among their drawings and inscriptions. Dogs were not just friends, they served a purpose: There were dogs to hunt birds, pull sleds, herd sheep, burrow after rats—even sit in laps! What your dog was originally bred to do influences the way it behaves. The American Kennel Club recognizes over 140 breeds, and there are hundreds more distinct breeds around the world. To make sense of the breeds, they are grouped according to their size or function. The AKC has seven groups:

1) Sporting, 2) Working,
3) Herding, 4) Hounds,
5) Terriers, 6) Toys,
7) Non-Sporting

Can you name a breed from each group? Here's some help: (1) Golden Retriever; (2) Doberman Pinscher; (3) Collie; (4) Beagle; (5) Scottish Terrier; (6) Maltese; and (7) Dalmatian. All modern domestic dogs (Canis familiaris) are related, however different they look, and are all descended from Canis lupus, the gray wolf.

How Guns Changed Dogs

Hunting changed forever with the invention of the flintlock gun, which had a short lag time between when the trigger was pulled and the contents shot from the muzzle. With that kind of weapon, all the hunter needed was the dog to find and flush the bird, then bring it back to him. To keep his job, the spaniel evolved from a field-beating crazy to a highly trainable hunting companion. This happened over the course of several hundred years.

As the hunter's needs changed, so did the spaniel's style, size and overall purpose. The writer Thomas Bewicke (1752–1828) was the first to distinguish the two types most popular today: the Springer and the Cocker Spaniels. Both were land spaniels. The Cocker or "cocking" spaniel was usually under twenty-five pounds in size, while "springing" and "setting" spaniels were larger. The springing spaniels became Springers, while the setting spaniels evolved into today's Setters (English, Irish and Gordon).

Settling on the Springer

By the late eighteenth/early nineteenth century, the Springer was well on its way to being the breed we know it as today. An Englishman by the name of Boughey kept a stud book for his kennel of Springers dating back to 1812. Thanks to his records, we know many Springers trace back to his dogs Mop I, Mop II and Frisk.

This Springer retrieves a bird for his master the way so many of his breed have done before him.

The Spaniel Club was founded in England in the late nineteenth century. Its members drafted a standard for the breed's physical conformation and began to show their dogs. What the "show" people were looking for wasn't always what the hunters agreed should be primary characteristics, and some hunters formed another club, the Sporting Spaniel Society. The latter organized tests of the Spaniels' hunting ability. Both held competitive field trials.

The English Kennel Club recognized the English Springer Spaniel as a distinct breed in 1902, and the first Springer field champion in the world was Rivington Sam, owned by C.A. Phillips. Many of today's Springers can trace back to Rivington Sam or to five other popular English sires: FC (Field Champion)

Velox Powder, Denne Duke, Dash of Hagley, Caistor Rex and Cornwallis Cavalier.

The Springer on American Shores

The spaniel, it turns out, is one of our country's earliest settlers. An entry in the *Journal of the Beginning of the English Plantation*, circa 1622, states that one of the pilgrims's spaniels chased deer. On a more reputable note, *The Sportsman's Companion*, a late eighteenth-century journal, described several varieties of spaniel as fine shooting dogs.

The American Spaniel Club was founded in 1880, in part to sort out and define the various types of spaniels. The most obvious criterion was size, and it was decided anything weighing over twenty-eight pounds was a Springer. The American Kennel Club (the "club of clubs," also the governing body for the sport of dogs) was founded in 1884 and registered the first Springer Spaniel twenty-six years later, in 1910—a bitch named Denne Lucy. The AKC currently recognizes seven breeds of spaniels in the Sporting Group:

> Cocker Spaniel (known in England as the American Cocker Spaniel)
>
> English Cocker Spaniel (known in England as the Cocker Spaniel)
>
> Clumber Spaniel
>
> American Water Spaniel
>
> Sussex Spaniel
>
> Welsh Springer Spaniel
>
> and, of course, English Springer Spaniel

Interestingly, the Irish Water Spaniel is considered a retriever even though the American Water Spaniel is not. The two breeds of Cockers and the two breeds of Springers are quite similar in appearance. The Cocker is more defined than the English Cocker, and the English Springer is more defined than its Welsh relative. Also, the Welshs are red and white, where the English are brown and white or black and white. Cockers come in a number of colors and color variations. Clumbers are predominantly white; Sussex and American Water predominantly brown. The American Spaniel Club is still active; theirs is the first dog show every year. All the spaniels listed above compete at that show.

A Club for the Breed

The first club for Springers was formed in 1924. It was the English Springer Spaniel Field Trial Association, and the ESSFTA remains the breed's parent club to this day. The club's aim has always been to further the breed in the field (working) and on the bench (showing). Between 1910 and 1922 the greatest activity in Springers in North America was in Canada, where Mr. Eudore Chevrier popularized the breed with his excellent hunting dog, Longbranch Teal.

The same year that the English Springer Spaniel Field Trial Association was formed, the breed's admirers held their first "specialty" show for Springers (a dog show featuring just this breed). It was in Englewood, New Jersey, 1922, and the dogs were field trial dogs whose owners worked them one day and showed them for conformation the next.

Springer fanciers enjoyed both field and show-ring pursuits with their dogs until the early 1930s. Around that time, breeders who were more interested in conformation became more aware of the overall appearance of the dog and less keen to subject their show dogs to the hazards of the field. A split in Springer "type" developed that is still evident.

A dog imported from England in 1928 had a very important impact on Springers in this country. He was Ch. Nuthill Dignity, a tri-international champion whose winnings included Best in Show at the

FAMOUS OWNERS OF ENGLISH SPRINGER SPANIELS

George Bush

Barbara Bush

Fatty Arbuckle

Vicki Lawrence

Patrick Muldoon

prestigious Westminster Kennel Club show in New York in 1930.

One of the Greats

The dog with the greatest influence on American English Springer Spaniel show dogs was American and English Ch. Rufton Recorder. Imported from England in 1933 by Mr. Fred Hunt of Devon, Pennsylvania, Recorder caused quite a stir when he first showed up in the ring. Hunt had imported him to continue his breeding program, and hadn't intended to show him, but he realized Recorder was the best Springer he'd ever seen.

English and American Champion Rufton Recorder, a dog with a tremendous influence on the history of the show Springer in the United States.

Recorder was taller and more compact than that day's dogs. He had straight forelegs, excellent feet, and striking markings that set him apart from his competitors. Recorder earned his American championship easily. He was bred to a daughter of Ch. Nuthill Dignity, Woodelf of Breeze, and produced the most famous litter in Springer history—a litter of six bench show champions. One of these dogs, Ch. Green Valley Punch, also earned his Field Championship in 1938, becoming an impressive Dual Champion. (Mr. Hunt himself handled the dog to both bench and field titles.) There hasn't been a dual champion Springer since.

Show vs. Field

The "split" in Springers, made so significantly obvious by the fact that the last dual championship was awarded the breed in 1938, is nothing new to Springer fanciers. One of today's top Springer breeders—and one of the most influential in the history of the breed—is Julia Gasow. In her book, *The New Complete English Springer Spaniel* (Howell Book House. New York: 1994, coauthored by Edward G. Roggenkamp III), Mrs. Gasow writes, "Many felt that this division would be the ruination of the breed, but results have proved quite the contrary. Each of the two phases has become so highly specialized that we now have English Springer Spaniel superiority on two fronts, as it were: ability unsurpassed by any other breed in field trials, and a bench record unmatched by any other breed since 1967."

Mrs. Julia Gasow with "Robert" after he won Best in Show at Westminster in 1993.

Today's Dog

It was one of Mrs. Gasow's dogs that was the Best in Show winner at the prestigious Westminster Kennel Club in 1993. The dog's name is Ch. Salilyn's Condor (familiarly known as "Robert"), a handsome liver-and-white Springer. Robert typifies the English Springer: fun-loving, athletic and gorgeous.

Big fans of the breed are former president George
Bush and his wife, Barbara. Their Springer, Millie,
became famous not just as a White House dog, but as a
White House mom, whelping a litter of puppies in the
White House. Millie would accompany President Bush
into the Oval Office almost every day, as did one of her
puppies, Ranger, who was the president's favorite.
Millie's book ("as told to" Barbara Bush), was a best-
seller in the 1980s.

The English Springer Spaniel is still actively used in
field work, and he's got a solid following at dog shows.
He's an able competitor in obedience trials, tracking
and agility, as well. His ancestors knew how to find food
for the table, and even though that's not a necessity
for the breed today, he can still do it well. But it's certainly on the home front that he excels, warming
hearts and laps alike.

chapter 3

The **World**
According to the
English Springer Spaniel

In Chapter 1 you learned that, according to the standard for the breed, the Springer's temperament is "friendly, eager to please, quick to learn, willing to obey." Sounds ideal, doesn't it? Before you start thinking your puppy is going to grow into a perfectly behaved, do-anything-for-you dog, let's

read between the lines and take a closer look at the dog we call the English Springer Spaniel.

The English Springer Spaniel is a medium-size, moderately active dog. He's large enough to be durable in a family with children, but not so large he won't be at home in an apartment in town. His size and happy-go-lucky attitude make him a good family pet—even if you're the only member of his "family."

Remember the Past

As you watch your puppy grow, or get to know your older dog, always remember what the Springer was originally bred for. This will tell you a lot about the way he responds to things. Remember that the Springer had to find and flush game for his master. That means he had to work out in front of the hunter, searching back and forth across the fields, nose slightly off the ground, waiting to get a whiff of quail or pheasant or dove or chukkar—any of a number of local gamebirds.

Your dog will especially enjoy activities you train for and do together, like agility. This Springer is bounding through the tire jump on an agility course.

When he'd get that delicious whiff, he'd stop in mid-run, keeping his focus intently on the area the smell was coming from, waiting for his master to join him. He'd wait until told by his master to move in, at which time he'd rush at the spot where he suspected the bird was hiding. This was usually enough to scare the bird, who would fly up out of the brush. The hunter would be ready and, with his eye on the target, fire a shot to bring the bird down. The Springer was expected to wait again and, if necessary, to go find the downed bird, scoop it gently into his mouth and return it to his master. Sometimes the Springer would have to retrieve the bird out in a pond. His master might hunt like this for several hours before returning home.

His Favorite Things

What do you expect some of your Springer's favorite things will be, based on his ancestry?

You can be sure he'll like to be with you and the other human "masters" in his family. He'll look to you for guidance, companionship and lots of shared pleasures, like long walks in the field.

He'll enjoy being outdoors, and will be especially happy running back and forth across open fields or sniffing along hedgerows. He wants to find birds for you! He doesn't mind water and he's not too particular about the weather in general. He'll stay out hunting with you all day if you want. He'll also be happy to head on home when you say it's time.

Your Springer will also like to retrieve things for you, and because he's been bred to have a "soft" mouth (meaning he carries things gently), the toy you send him to get shouldn't come back destroyed.

Don't Neglect Guidance

There is one very important element in your relationship with your Springer that will enable you both to fully enjoy your time together. That one thing is guidance. Your Springer needs to know his limits, and you have to teach him. With his intense desire to serve you, he will feel lost without boundaries and fair rules.

A DOG'S SENSES

Sight: With their eyes located farther apart than ours, dogs can detect movement at a greater distance than we can, but they can't see as well up close. They can also see better in less light, but can't distinguish many colors.

Sound: Dogs can hear about four times better than we can, and they can hear high-pitched sounds especially well. Their ancestors, the wolves, howled to let other wolves know where they were; our dogs do the same, but they have a wider range of vocalizations, including barks, whimpers, moans and whines.

Smell: A dog's nose is his greatest sensory organ. His sense of smell is so great he can follow a trail that's weeks old, detect odors diluted to one-millionth the concentration we'd need to notice them, even sniff out a person under water!

Taste: Dogs have fewer taste buds than we do, so they're likelier to try anything—and usually do, which is why it's especially important for their owners to monitor their food intake. Dogs are omnivores, which means they eat meat as well as vegetable matter like grasses and weeds.

Touch: Dogs are social animals and love to be petted, groomed and played with.

A Springer without household rules is a dog who will soon be in trouble. Not because he's a bad dog, but because he doesn't know what you want from him.

Let's look at it from his point of view again. He wants to be with you. He wants to share your activities. So what will he do if he's not given guidance? He will follow you around the house everywhere you go, every time you go from one side of the room to the other.

The misguided Springer will be snuffling around for the scent of something pleasing, and once he finds it, he'll want it. That's great if you're hunting down birds, but what if you're eating potato chips? Do you want a dog who's been bred to be persistent following after you, waiting to share in your "kill," wondering when it's going to be his turn? Pair this kind of behavior with his soulful eyes, and you have the makings of a die-hard begger.

Springer Spaniels can be boisterous. As energetic youngsters, they may knock down small children to get what they want. They can also be mouthy when young, and you want to be sure they have a supply of appropriate chew toys so they don't take the need out on your arm or your furniture.

This dog is having a "howling" good time dressed up at a dog show.

Training Works Wonders

The breed standard wouldn't say it if it weren't true, and the Springer's "eager to please, quick to learn" nature makes him a great dog to work with.

Yes, your puppy and your dog will do things you aren't crazy about, but you'll find he will be happy to learn what it is you want him to do instead! The time you spend training him will be rewarding for both of you.

30

Take your puppy to a special Puppy Kindergarten where he'll have the chance to interact with a lot of other dogs his age. He'll be in a strange place with strange dogs (and people)—all the more reason to look to you for guidance and reassurance. Puppies as young as a few months can be taught to sit using small bits of their favorite foods, like cheese. (See Chapter 8 for more on training.)

This Springer is participating in a Hunting Test. His handler is about to send him into the field to look for birds. This was the breed's original purpose.

As your puppy grows, or if you're starting with an older dog, enroll in a basic obedience class. Like the Puppy Kindergarten, it'll be a positive experience for him in that he'll meet other dogs, and a good one for you because you'll automatically be the one he'll look to for leadership. You'll learn how to teach your dog to sit, lie down, stay and walk nicely by your side on a leash. What a great dog! And what a great owner. By letting your dog know what you want him to do, you're taking the responsibility off of him to choose what he should do and putting it onto you—his leader. Doesn't mean he'll never do anything you don't want him to, but those times will be fewer.

Common Questions

These are the questions new or potential owners of Springers ask me most often about what it's like to live with these dogs. Since I've been doing it for nearly thirty years, I feel I can answer honestly. Keep in mind that all dogs are individuals; yours may be a little more or less like I describe.

WHAT ARE THE GOOD THINGS ABOUT THE BREED?

Springers are medium-size. They're athletic enough to enjoy being out with their owners all day but not so energetic they need hours of walking every day.

They're good family dogs, especially families with children in the age eight to twelve range who want a buddy to play with and a pal to curl up with.

They get along well with each other and with other dogs.

They are not aggressive and they are not shy; they are very gentle.

The "show" Springers, like this one, are a bit heavier and squarer than their field-bred siblings.

WHAT ARE THE BAD THINGS ABOUT THE BREED?

Springers aren't extremely hairy, but they do shed. They are not for people who mind dog hair around the house or who don't want to bother with regular coat care.

They can be boisterous and mouthy when young.

They are very people-oriented and won't accept being left alone for very long stretches of time.

The breed is prone to some hereditary problems that owners should know about, like progressive retinal atrophy, retinal dysplasia and aggressive temperament, sometimes incorrectly referred to as "rage syndrome." (See Chapter 7 for more on these conditions and others particular to the ESS.)

HOW MUCH AND HOW OFTEN DO THEY NEED TO BE EXERCISED?

The great thing about Springers is that they don't require a great deal of exercise. They like it, and they're happy to go out with you, but a lot of exercise is not a requirement to keep these dogs happy. Once they're past the puppy stage, most are perfectly content to be couch potatoes.

ARE THEY GOOD WITH KIDS?

Yes, especially in the age range of eight years and up, or if they grow up with them. You should always supervise a dog with a small child or infant. Children may pull on ears or poke eyes or step on feet by accident and really hurt a dog, who may react in self-defense by nipping. Springers are consistently reliable even in such instances, but you're always better safe than sorry.

You can see by the look in this dog's eyes that he's gentle, good-natured and eager to please—all great things about the English Springer.

WHAT'S THE DIFFERENCE BETWEEN THE SHOW TYPES AND THE FIELD TYPES?

The show types are more typically bought as pets because they're a bit bigger and some are a bit mellower. The field types can be really laid-back or really high-energy, and a pet owner should ask about the parents and speak with the breeder at length if he wants a field-type Springer. Show Springers can make fine "gentleman" hunters, but so can the field types. In appearance, the field types are smaller, finer-boned, carry less coat and are predominantly white rather than "blanketed" in patches of color.

HOW MUCH GROOMING DOES THIS BREED NEED?

English Springers need routine coat care—that means brushing at least once a week and some trimming. They don't need baths very often; dirt brushes right out. Their ears are prone to infection since they're long and hairy, so they need regular inspecting and care. Depending on how "neat" you want your Springer to look, he'll need to go to the groomer for a professional trim every two or three months. (Grooming is covered thoroughly in Chapter 6.)

WHAT ABOUT THE MEDICAL PROBLEMS?

Like other pure breeds of dogs, Springers suffer from some genetic problems. These include hip dysplasia, retinal dysplasia and progressive retinal atrophy. All of these are discussed in detail in Chapter 7.

What's important is to ask the person from whom you got your puppy about the puppy's parents, grandparents and as many other relatives as possible. Did any of these dogs suffer these conditions? Does the breeder check his or her dogs for those diseases at the appropriate times? If you're still not sure, ask to speak to his or her veterinarian. If the seller gives you a lot of excuses or says you can't, take it as a warning sign.

And remember, dogs whose relatives are perfectly healthy may end up having a hereditary disease. If your dog develops any of these hereditary conditions, make sure you tell the person who sold you the dog, and do what you can for your dog.

WHAT IS THE TYPICAL LIFESPAN OF A SPRINGER?

Springers typically live to be twelve to fifteen years old.

The Hunting Springer

A chapter on the world according to the Springer that didn't say something about the breed's hunting prowess would be incomplete. With that in mind, we're including this excerpt from Julia Gasow and Edward K. Roggenkamp III's book *The New Complete English Springer Spaniel* (Howell Book House, 1994).

"Noted authorities such as the noted dog writer David Michael Duffy . . . and others generally concede that of all types of gun dogs, the English Springer Spaniel is a leading contender for the title of all-around gun dog for the one-dog-sportsman who wants to hunt upland game and waterfowl. Having hunted and shot over many dogs of the several breeds and types over the years, I agree completely. English Springer Spaniels are great all-around dogs. They can do almost anything—some things better than others—but almost anything.

> **CHARACTERISTICS OF THE ENGLISH SPRINGER SPANIEL**
>
> happy-go-lucky attitude
>
> eager to please
>
> quick to learn
>
> boisterous and mouthy when young
>
> doesn't require a great deal of exercise

"As Charles Goodall explained it back in the 1950s: 'The properly bred, well trained and experienced Springer Spaniel is a joy to gun over. He should walk obediently at heel without leash, and when ordered to hunt will fairly explode, and always in the direction in which he is sent (right or left of the gunner). . . . A real sportsman who thinks the hunt is equally as important as the quantity of game brought home will never hunt without a trained gun dog. The Springer is the pheasant dog par excellence.'

"But consider this: Spaniels, by their nature, hunt with the hunter. That means you will be in the cover with the dog. In today's world of exercise, jogging, hiking, workouts and health concerns, the spaniel is an active dog for sporting shooters. Springers will give you plenty of warning by their body language and tail action, but you won't often have time to plant your feet, shoulder the gun and get set. This is snap shooting at its best; tremendous fun for true sports and a game of fast, exciting action."

MORE INFORMATION ON ENGLISH SPRINGER SPANIELS

NATIONAL BREED CLUB

English Springer Spaniel Field Trial Association
Ms. Karen Koopman, Corresponding Secretary
347 5th Avenue, Ste. 1406
New York, NY 10016

The club can send you information on all aspects of the breed, including the names and addresses of breed clubs in your area, as well as obedience and field trial clubs. Inquire about membership.

BOOKS

Gasow, Julia F. and Edward K. Roggenkamp III. *The New Complete English Springer Spaniel.* New York: Howell Book House, 1994.

Nicholas, Anna Katherine. *The Book of the English Springer Spaniel.* Neptune, NJ: TFH, 1983.

MAGAZINES

English Springer Spaniel Quarterly
P.O. Box 1247
Chesapeake, VA 23327

Spaniels in the Field
10714 Escondido Dr.
Cincinnati, OH 45249

VIDEOS

American Kennel Club, *English Springer Spaniels.*

Living

with an

part two

English Springer Spaniel

chapter 4

Bringing Your
English Springer
Spaniel
Home

One of the first things you will need to do when you bring your Springer puppy home is choose a name for it. You don't know much about the dog your puppy will become, so you don't have a lot to go on. Use your imagination. Make sure it's not a name you will be embarrassed to call out across the park.

Once you decide on a name, don't change your mind. This will confuse the puppy. Use the name you have chosen for her, and call her name when you address her, praise her or when you are looking at her. Don't use lots of cute nicknames at first. Use her name in a friendly, cheerful tone of voice and she will start to respond to it very quickly.

Your Puppy's Veterinarian

Choosing the right veterinarian is important for both your dog's health and your peace of mind. If you got your Springer from someone close by, ask that person to suggest a veterinarian. If you're not comfortable doing that, or you want to explore your options first, try contacting a local ESS club (you can get the address from the national club, listed after Chapter 3) and speaking to some of its members. Talk to other dog owners in the neighborhood, or call some veterinarians in the area and feel them out over the phone.

When you visit a prospective veterinarian, pay attention to the office environment. Is the staff friendly? The waiting area clean and comfortable? Are you kept waiting for an unreasonable amount of time with no explanation? When you meet the veterinarian, is he or she courteous and thorough? Remember, your vet should be someone with whom you can speak frankly and easily about your animal's health. You shouldn't feel like you are being rushed out of the office with unanswered questions. Your vet should have respect for your observations, and treat your dog gently and carefully. If you think your vet is being too rough or ignoring problems, consider finding another vet.

You, too, have a responsibility to build a good relationship with your veterinarian. Educate yourself so you can ask the appropriate questions and understand the answers he or she gives you. Also, understand that the veterinarian's time may be very short and it may be more productive for you to ask follow-up questions of the veterinary technician or attendant. Good communication between you and the staff is the best possible thing for your dog.

Don't wait until you bring your puppy home to choose your vet. Your puppy should visit the vet's soon after you acquire her to make sure all is in good order. Most breeders will make that initial visit part of your agreement with them. Your veterinarian will want to put your puppy on a schedule for vaccinations and regular check-ups. So start getting recommendations and

**PUPPY
ESSENTIALS**

Your new
puppy will
need:

food bowl

water bowl

collar

leash

I.D. tag

bed

crate

toys

grooming
supplies

setting up appointments weeks before you plan to bring your Springer home.

What Your Puppy Will Need

Once you've picked your puppy and determined the day you'll bring her home, you will have to get ready for the new arrival. Purchase some essential supplies before you bring your puppy home; that way you won't have to dash out and leave your puppy alone and unattended.

FOOD AND WATER BOWLS

Your puppy will need separate bowls for food and water. There are many kinds available, and this is largely a matter of personal choice. Do remember, however, that puppies have a tendency to play with everything, including food and water, so it might be a good idea to get at least the water dish in a heavy ceramic style. This is,

Make sure you have puppy-friendly toys for your dog to play with.

of course, no guarantee he will not make a mess of it, but it will help ensure that your puppy doesn't go without water because he has tipped over his bowl and you haven't noticed.

Make sure your puppy has fresh water available at all times, and if he does have a tendency to tip over his bowl, check it often to make sure it's full. There are bowls designed especially for dogs with long ears. They are narrower at the top than the bottom; thus, the dog's ears do not get in the water or food as much.

COLLAR AND LEASH

You will also need a lightweight leather or nylon collar with a buckle for your ESS puppy. Nylon may be preferable at this age, as puppies like to chew on leather. Do not use a chain choke collar until the puppy is older, and even then only use it for training sessions. It can get caught on any number of things, including the puppy's own crate, and literally choke her.

A collar should fit well, but not tightly. You should be able to slip two fingers between the collar and the puppy's neck. Check the collar as the puppy grows. You will have to loosen it every once in a while and probably replace it a couple of times before your puppy's neck is full grown.

Your puppy will also need a leash. Again, a lightweight nylon one may be best to keep your puppy from gnawing on it as you try to walk her. The leather ones may also be a bit heavy for a small puppy. Graduate to a nicer leash when the puppy is older and you can be sure the leash won't turn into a snack.

To introduce the leash, put it on the puppy for a few minutes at a time and let him walk around with it, dragging it along behind him. He will start to get used to the way it feels and he won't balk when you start to lead him on it. (See Chapter 8, Basic Training.)

TOYS

Make sure your puppy has plenty of toys she knows are hers, though there will certainly be times when she prefers your expensive shoes to her rawhide bone. Old stuffed animals are great for chewing on and snuggling with, but make sure the plastic eyes or any other parts that could be chewed off and swallowed are removed. Chew toys, such as large rawhide bones or hard plastic ones, are great for gnawing; tennis balls, of course, are great fun to retrieve and chase. You can also make toys by tying a knot in an old sock, or giving your puppy the cardboard from a used roll of paper towels.

Try to avoid the soft plastic toys with the squeaker in the center. A puppy's teeth will easily break the plastic and they can choke on the small squeaker inside. Also steer clear of small balls your puppy can choke on.

Puppies will turn just about anything into a toy. Try to make sure it's not something you want to keep.

IDENTIFICATION

No matter how safe and secure your yard is, or how good you are about using a leash, your puppy can easily get loose and get lost. Make sure that if your puppy is separated from you, you have a chance of being reunited with her. She needs some form of identification.

The puppy should have an ID tag on the collar with her name, your name and your phone number. If

someone finds your dog, they can call and tell you.

Other possibilities are a tattoo or a microchip. Dogs are tattooed on their inner thighs with their owner's social security number or their registration number. The tattoo number is registered with an organization like the National Dog Registry. If your dog is lost and the finder calls a shelter or veterinarian, someone at that facility may report the number and the organization will track you down.

This puppy has an identification tag secured onto her collar.

The microchip is a rice-size pellet that's encoded with your dog's information (your name, address and phone) and injected under the skin between a dog's shoulder blades. This chip can be scanned and read by machines available in some animal shelters and vet hospitals. The advantage is that, unlike a collar, your dog cannot lose it. The disadvantage is that, although this may prove useful in the future, the machinery needed to read it is not readily available. Right now, it's not the only means you should use to identify your dog.

Though you may want to consider the microchip and the tattoo, I urge you to also use a simple ID tag. The machinery used to read the microchip is not widely available, and a tattoo is only helpful if a person knows where to look for it and what it means. If your dog gets out of your yard and is found by a neighbor, a likely scenario, a microchip or tattoo would be useless.

PUPPY FOOD

Ask the person you bought your puppy from what kind of food your puppy has been eating. Feed your puppy this food for the first few days after she arrives home.

If you want to switch food, do it gradually, adding a little bit more each day to the regular food. (See Chapter 5, "Feeding Your English Springer Spaniel," for complete information on feeding your puppy.)

A CRATE IS GREAT

Your puppy will need a crate. Some people think of crates as cages and won't consider them for their dogs. What they don't understand is that, if used correctly, the crate is both a place of refuge for a puppy (and a dog) as well as a wonderful training aid for you and your family.

Choose a crate that is big enough for her to stand up and turn around in comfortably, but not one that's too big or she will use one end to sleep in and the other end as a potty. Put the crate somewhere that will be the dog's space—some place she can rest undisturbed, but not some place completely removed from the family. Remember, your puppy is a social animal, and

---

HOUSEHOLD DANGERS

Curious puppies and inquisitive dogs get into trouble not because they are bad, but simply because they want to investigate the world around them. It's our job to protect our dogs from harmful substances, like the following:

IN THE HOUSE

cleaners, especially pine oil

perfumes, colognes, aftershaves

medications, vitamins

office and craft supplies

electric cords

chicken or turkey bones

chocolate

some house and garden plants, like ivy, oleander and poinsettia

IN THE GARAGE

antifreeze

garden supplies, like snail and slug bait, pesticides, fertilizers, mouse and rat poisons

---

45

being too far away from her family will make her very uneasy.

If you introduce the crate in the proper way, it will become a haven your dog goes to willingly. Put a soft, snuggly blanket in the crate and a toy or two. At first entice her into the crate with a treat, and allow her to explore it without shutting the door. Let her wander in and out, sniffing out the place. After a little while, gently shut the door when she's inside, and leave her in for just a few minutes. Let her out after a little while as long as she's not crying and complaining. If she is, just ignore her and keep her in there until she's calmed down, then let her out.

Don't pay any attention to her while she's crying, even though it will be very difficult. As soon as her cries taper off, let her out. Don't let yourself think you're being a bad owner when you put her in the crate; your puppy is sure to pick up on your misgivings and she'll be convinced you're doing something bad, which will make her complain all the more. Make going into the crate a positive experience and your puppy will learn it is.

The crate is a great training tool for housebreaking. Your puppy will not soil the place she sleeps in if she can help it, though you must be able to let her out regularly for this to work. The crate also helps to give you peace of mind when you have to leave your puppy home alone. In the crate, she can't do any damage to your rugs or furniture.

Never leave the puppy in a crate for more than a few hours at a time, and never use the crate for punishment. If you do go out and leave the puppy in her crate, be sure to return and let your puppy out to relieve herself. Puppies don't have big bladders and they'll try their hardest not to soil their crate. You have to make sure someone is home to let the puppy out often.

Puppy in the House

To help train your dog and to make it easier on your house, it's best if you keep your dog confined to one or two rooms while she is still little. These should be the rooms where the family is most likely to be, where she can be around people all the time. This way you can keep an eye on her; she'll be able to "tell" you when she needs to relieve herself, and you can make sure she's not getting into mischief. If she has the run of the house, there's no telling what she'll be up to at any given moment. Also, you will want to be with your puppy, because that's why you got her.

Make a Schedule for Your Puppy

Puppies thrive on schedules. It makes their totally new world a little more predictable and secure. They can thrive and explore knowing that their basic needs will be taken care of regularly by people they trust. The schedule will help you, too, because you will know when your puppy needs to go out. If you take her out when she needs to go out, housebreaking is that much easier.

Your puppy will look forward to the times you go out together.

Your puppy will need to go out after eating, exercising and after waking in the morning or after a nap. So take your puppy out first thing in the morning. Then feed her. Feed your puppy at the same times each day. Take her out again after feeding her, then spend some time playing with her. She'll need a nap next. And after the nap? You've got it— she'll need to go out. Then be fed. Then out, play, nap, etc.

In no time you'll have a consistent schedule developed. Your puppy will get excited around the time she knows you usually go out. She can expect it and look forward to it, and that makes it all the more fun for her.

When planning your puppy's schedule, make sure there's lots of time in it for your puppy to play and be with you and your family. Dogs are social creatures and thrive on interaction and companionship. Try not to leave them alone for too long, or they will devise other ways to get your attention.

While planning your puppy's schedule, look closely at your own. Do you have enough time to spend with your new puppy? If you and your partner work, is there someone who can come in the middle of the day and let her out, walk her and spend time with her? Do you have obligations in the evening that prevent you from being with your puppy, grooming, playing, or snuggling? Remember that puppies need lots of attention. Ask yourself if you are ready to make the lifestyle adjustment that getting a puppy requires.

Your puppy will be happy to chew on your nice boots if you don't provide an appropriate chew toy.

Puppy-Proofing Your Home

When you are home you cannot watch your puppy every minute. Like an inquisitive toddler, she will get into mischief the moment you turn your back. It's up to you to keep things that are potentially dangerous out of her way, where they cannot hurt her. Out of the way means locked where she cannot get to them, not on top of the counter. You will be surprised at how ath-letic puppies can be.

Make sure you've secured electrical outlets and dan-gling cords, which puppies may find fun to chew on. Make sure household chemicals are up where your puppy can't get them. This especially applies to antifreeze, which is extremely dangerous and which dogs seem to like the taste of. Take pill bottles off your bedside table and put them securely away. Puppies like the sound of the pills rolling inside the bottle and they can easily chew a hole through a plastic bottle and ingest the medicine. Check your yard and make sure insecticides, fertilizers and other chemical products are stored safely away.

Keep an eye on your puppy to keep him from snacking on things that may be bad for him.

Check the house for poisonous plants, including ivy, poinsettia and oleander. Put these up where your puppy can't get them. If they are outside, try to keep your puppy in a separate part of the yard.

If you have an enclosed yard your ESS can play in, check once more to make sure it's secure. Check the gate to make sure it cannot be easily pushed open, and the fence to make sure he cannot easily get under-neath it.

Put all personal items out of the puppy's reach. Toys, videos, books and everything else you don't want the puppy to get should be stored up high or inside closed containers. Remind other members of the family not to leave things on the floor. Shoes seem especially attractive to teething puppies.

Consider an Older Dog

If you don't think you can cope with a puppy, or don't have the time and energy to spend training and keeping up with one, investigate the possibilities of getting an older Springer. Contact the parent club for the name and address of their breed rescue coordinator (see "More Information on English Springer Spaniels," between Chapters 3 and 4 for the address of the parent club). That person can tell you about older dogs who need homes.

When bringing an older dog into the home, you must give her time to adjust and become familiar with her new surroundings. She is not as flexible as a puppy, and may take a little longer getting used to things. As with your puppy, do everything you can to make her comfortable in her new environment. Offer her a soft bed, plenty of toys and, most of all, lots of attention. Springers are friendly and even-tempered, and after a few days your new-old dog should be starting to fit right in.

chapter 5

Feeding
Your
English Springer
Spaniel

The importance of good nutrition cannot be emphasized enough. The food your dog eats contains vital substances that give him energy, create healthy coat and bones, keep the immune system strong, and fight infections—in short, everything he needs to grow strong and healthy. Your

dog's food should have the nutrients he needs in a formula in which his body can digest them, and in the proper amounts.

What to Feed Your Springer

There are so many different commercial foods on the market today. They vary in content, packaging, cost and quality. How do you choose the one that's best for your dog?

It's true that dogs can get by on a lot less than the best. In fact, it's amazing how very little dogs (and people, for that matter) need to just survive. However, you want him to *thrive*, have a healthy coat and clear, alert eyes, be active and energetic, and live a long and healthy life. He can't do these things on a substandard food. To make sure your dog is getting the nutrition he needs, don't cut corners. This doesn't mean you have to go gourmet, just choose a high-quality food that has meats and grains among the most plentiful ingredients.

TYPES OF FOODS/TREATS

There are three types of commercially available dog food—dry, canned and semimoist—and a huge assortment of treats (lucky dogs!) to feed your dog. Which should you choose?

Dry and canned foods contain similar ingredients. The primary difference between them is their moisture content. The moisture is not just water. It's blood and broth, too, the very things that dogs adore. So while canned food is more palatable, dry food is more economical, convenient and effective in controlling tartar buildup. Most owners feed a 25% canned/75% dry diet to give their dogs the benefit of both. Just be sure your dog is getting the nutrition he needs (you and your veterinarian can determine this).

Semimoist foods have the flavor dogs love and the convenience owners want. However, they tend to contain excessive amounts of artificial colors and preservatives.

Dog treats come in every size, shape and flavor imaginable, from organic cookies shaped like postmen to beefy chew sticks. Dogs seem to love them all, so enjoy the variety. Just be sure not to overindulge your dog. Factor treats into her regular meal sizes.

Dry or Canned Food?

Nutritionally complete dry and canned foods are both available. Most dry foods are formulated to be nutritionally complete, while some canned foods are meant to be mixed with dry food.

I do not recommend that you feed your dog solely canned food, even if it is a nutritionally complete kind. Canned food is moist and soft, and does not help clean your dog's teeth the way dry food does. If you want to give your dog canned for flavor and palatability, a good combination is two-thirds dry dog food with one-third canned dog food.

Water

It may seem obvious to mention that your dog needs water, but it can't be emphasized enough. Like people, dogs can go for days without food, but they need water every day. Check your dog's bowl often and make sure he always has a supply of clean fresh water. If your puppy or dog has had diarrhea, be especially attentive to his water supply. Diarrhea is extremely dehydrating.

What's in Your Dog's Food?

When it comes to choosing a food for your puppy or adult dog, there are many good-quality commercial dog foods available, formulated for all different sizes, ages and activity levels. It is probably much simpler to stick with a commercial dog food than to try to cook for your dog yourself. Dog food companies spend thousands and thousands of dollars to maximize nutrition for your dog.

Make sure your dog always has a supply of fresh, clean water along with high-quality food.

Nutritionally complete dog food should include the elements your dog needs to be healthy and active. These are protein, carbohydrates, fats, vitamins, minerals and water.

Protein is the building block of tissues. It is acquired primarily from meats. Growing puppies and active dogs need extra protein, and puppy formulas and foods for active dogs are designed to provide it.

Carbohydrates provide energy and aid digestion. They are stored in the body until they are needed, unlike protein which needs to be replenished daily. Examples of carbohydrates are grains and vegetables.

Fats are a source of energy and also contribute to a shiny coat and healthy skin. Too much fat, of course, will be stored under the skin and will make your Springer obese. Fat content should be monitored, and avoid giving fatty foods as snacks or treats.

Vitamins are necessary to aid and regulate bodily processes such as growth and immunity. Vitamin deficiencies can mean a lackluster coat, weight loss, unhealthy skin and vision problems. If you are feeding a high-quality dry dog food, it probably has all the vitamins your dog ordinarily needs.

TO SUPPLEMENT OR NOT TO SUPPLEMENT?

If you're feeding your dog a diet that's correct for her developmental stage and she's alert, healthy-looking and neither over- nor underweight, you don't need to add supplements. These include table scraps as well as vitamins and minerals. In fact, a growing puppy is in danger of developing musculoskeletal disorders by oversupplementation. If you have any concerns about the nutritional quality of the food you're feeding, discuss them with your veterinarian.

And more vitamins are not better! Too much can be as bad for your dog's health as too little, so do not add vitamins to your dog's diet unless your veterinarian recommends it.

One exception to the no-supplement rule is the possible use of vitamin C. Some claim it contributes to a healthy immune system, and when given to puppies can help potential problems (such as hip displaysia) be averted. It is a water-soluble vitamin, so it cannot hurt your puppy; if he doesn't need it, it will simply be passed out of the body in the urine. The allegedly great achievements of vitamin C are fairly controversial, however, so check with your veterinarian before starting any course of supplementation.

Minerals Like vitamins, minerals are necessary for your dog's body to function correctly and efficiently. They too are completely represented in good-quality commercial dog food.

To find out what's in your dog's food, **read labels.** See the sidebar on reading labels in this chapter. Be wary if ingredients like "by-products" appear near the top of the list. This is a cheap way to fulfill the protein requirements, and many of the ingredients in by-products, such as beaks, feathers, feet or hair, may not be digestible by your dog and are therefore totally useless.

Feeding Your Puppy

As we discussed in Chapter 4, it's best to start your puppy out with the same food the breeder had him on. He has enough stimulation to contend with in his new environment and doesn't need the added upset of new food. If you decide to change his food, do so gradually, adding a bit more each day until the switch has been made. This way he can adjust slowly, and you'll both be spared his diarrhea or upset stomach.

Puppies have little stomachs, but they are active and are growing very fast. Puppies should be fed small meals often, with a larger percentage of protein than for a normal adult dog. Growth requires extra protein for building new body tissue, and puppies are growing at a very rapid rate.

Feed your puppy four times a day until he is about three months old, then three times a day until he is five months. From five months to a year, two meals a day, one in the morning and one in the evening, are sufficient. Remember to increase his portions as he grows; he will need more food less often.

Don't "free-feed" your dog, which means putting all the food in the bowl for the day and letting him eat it when he wants. This encourages a

HOW TO READ THE DOG FOOD LABEL

With so many choices on the market, how can you be sure you are feeding the right food for your dog? The information is all there on the label—if you know what you're looking for.

Look for the nutritional claim right up top. Is the food "100% nutritionally complete"? If so, it's for nearly all life stages; "growth and maintenance," on the other hand, is for early development; puppy foods are marked as such, as are foods for senior dogs.

Ingredients are listed in descending order by weight. The first three or four ingredients will tell you the bulk of what the food contains. Look for the highest-quality ingredients, like meats and grains, to be among them.

The Guaranteed Analysis tells you what levels of protein, fat, fiber and moisture are in the food, in that order. While these numbers are meaningful, they won't tell you much about the quality of the food. Nutritional value is in the dry matter, not the moisture content.

In many ways, seeing is believing. If your dog has bright eyes, a shiny coat, a good appetite and a good energy level, chances are his diet's fine. Your dog's breeder and your veterinarian are good sources of advice if you're still confused.

finicky eater. Also, you want your dog to look to you for his meals. Put the amount you need into the bowl and place it on the floor for your dog. If he doesn't finish in fifteen to twenty minutes, pick up what's left and throw it away. Don't feed him again until dinnertime—and I mean nothing. At dinnertime, do the same thing. If your dog is healthy, he'll be eager to eat his entire meal when it's given to him. If he's not, it could be a sign something's bothering him, and the sooner you know about a health problem, the better.

Growing puppies and active adults need extra protein in their diets to give them the strength they need.

Feeding Your Adult Dog

Now that you've decreased mealtimes to twice a day, it's important for you to make sure your dog is getting all the nutritional components he needs in those two meals.

Your active dog will still need lots of protein. The body tissues that get broken down in the course of extra activity will need protein to be rebuilt every day. If your ESS is a hunting companion, for example, he will probably need a diet higher in protein. Look for a food formulated for especially active dogs.

Less active dogs will need less protein and fewer calories. Commercial dog foods that fit this lifestyle are also available.

Older dogs will need less food as their activity level declines.

What Not to Feed Your Dog

It's not a good idea to feed your Springer scraps from your own meals. People food is often fatty, greasy and spicy and can upset your dog's stomach.

It's definitely not a good idea to feed him from the table, as ESSs are inveterate thieves when it comes to food. The more encouragement you give them the worse they'll be. If you feed them from your plate, they think it's their right to help themselves if you happen to be ignoring them!

Whatever you do, *never* give your dog chocolate (even small amounts can be deadly for dogs) or bits of sweets or candy. They don't really like it anymore than they like anything else. In addition it's not good for their teeth, and has no nutritional value.

Snacks and Treats

Keep a can of dry dog biscuits to be used as treats. These are great to use when training or as a snack between meals, in the afternoon or before bed. Hard biscuits are good for your dog's teeth, and will help control tartar.

HOW MANY MEALS A DAY?

Individual dogs vary in how much they should eat to maintain a desired body weight—not too fat, but not too thin. Puppies need several meals a day, while older dogs may need only one. Determine how much food keeps your adult dog looking and feeling her best. Then decide how many meals you want to feed with that amount. Like us, most dogs love to eat, and offering two meals a day is more enjoyable for them. If you're worried about overfeeding, make sure you measure correctly and abstain from adding tidbits to the meals.

Whether you feed one or two meals, only leave your dog's food out for the amount of time it takes her to eat it—10 minutes, for example. Freefeeding (when food is available any time) and leisurely meals encourage picky eating. Don't worry if your dog doesn't finish all her dinner in the allotted time. She'll learn she should.

Other healthy treats you can feed your dog include bits of vegetables and fruits like carrots, steamed broccoli or beans, grapes, melon or apples. Cottage cheese and hard-boiled eggs are also good for your dog—in moderation, of course, and combined with a high-quality dog food. If you do feed your dog healthy people food, mix in a bit of it with his food as a special treat. Do not offer it every night, or he may pick out the yummy stuff and leave the dog food.

Above all, keep the number of snacks you offer your Springer low. Many American dogs are obese from overfeeding and lack of exercise. Instead of using snacks to show your dog how much you love him, take him for a walk or throw a ball. Offer healthy treats on occasion, and always lots of praise.

Grooming
Your
English Springer Spaniel

Your English Springer Spaniel requires regular grooming care to keep her looking her best. However, grooming not only keeps your English Springer Spaniel looking fine, but is also necessary for your dog's good health.

Ticks, burrs and other threats can be hiding in your English Springer Spaniel's long coat, and only regular brushing will alleviate that problem. A Springer's ears are

long and thick and need cleaning often. These dogs certainly require more grooming attention than a short-coated breed, but don't let that dissuade you. Grooming sessions are a good opportunity to bond with your dog and spend time with her.

Setting Up

A flat, raised surface is helpful, though not necessary, for home grooming sessions. It will save strain on your back if you otherwise have to bend down to reach your dog.

You will need some supplies as well. Pin brush, comb, straight scissors, cotton balls and witch hazel for ear cleaning, and teeth cleaning equipment are must-haves, even for the novice. You may also want to invest in a pair of clippers for trimming the hair on the ears.

Your Springer may get ticks and burrs caught in his coat after being outdoors. It's important to comb and brush him regularly.

Combing and Brushing

Brushing and combing your English Springer Spaniel often is essential, not only for top looks, but for health and cleanliness. Many nasty things, including prickers and ticks, will hide in your Springer's long coat.

First, start with a pin brush, which looks like a woman's hairbrush, and brush the coat well, from head to toe. This will help to remove old hair and any larger objects stuck in the coat. After you've brushed through the coat thoroughly, comb the hair through the undercoat to the skin. Take care not to catch any abra-sions on the skin that you can't see through the coat. If you feel something hard, don't comb through it, as-suming it is matted hair; feel it with your fingers to make sure it's not a wart or an old cut. Combing gets all the way through the coat and gives your Springer a fin-ished look.

If brushing and comb-ing are done gently and affectionately, he will grow to enjoy it. It can be a relaxing task for you as well, and gives you a chance to bond with your pet. You can do it while you are watching TV or helping the kids with their homework. It's a good opportunity for you to get your hands on your dog and feel for anything strange. See Chapter 7 for more information on what you should be looking for.

Brush your English Springer Spaniel's teeth regularly to keep his smile looking wonderful.

Tooth Care

While this part of grooming your dog may not be the most fun, it is necessary. Your dog's teeth accumulate tartar like ours do, and just like us, dogs require proper dental care or they will be subject to gum dis-ease and tooth loss as they age. Gum disease is not only painful, but the infection can actually be deadly when transmitted to other organs.

Brush your dog's teeth at least once a week. Use either a toothbrush made for dogs, or wrap a piece of gauze around your finger and scrub with that. Never use human toothpaste: some of the ingredients can be harmful to dogs. Instead, use a special canine formula toothpaste, or a baking soda solution.

While you brush the teeth, check for plaque build-up and signs of gum disease. These include red or swollen gums, foul breath and perhaps excessive drooling.

Follow up your own cleaning with a more thorough cleaning at the vet's. You should schedule a professional cleaning about once a year. The vet will usually sedate your dog, and use a scaler to scrape off accumulated plaque.

Trimming Nails

All dogs' nails have to be clipped, though an active dog's will require attention less often than those of a couch potato. If you hear nails clicking on the floor, they are too long and need to be cut.

Because of their long, furry ears, Springers need extra special care to keep the insides free of dirt and infection.

Start this procedure when your dog is a puppy. The sooner you introduce him to the sensation of having his feet handled, the less trouble it will be as he grows older. Many dogs don't like to have their feet touched and look as though this procedure is making them very uncomfortable. Don't worry, it's not as bad as they want you to think it is. And remember that it has to be done. Overgrown toenails can dig into the feet making movement awkward and painful.

The best tool to use is guillotine nail clippers, which accomplish the job more quickly, and thus more easily. Cut your dog's toenails under bright light so you can see the quick. Cut the nail above the quick (toward the tip of the nail). If you do accidentally cut too far down your dog will yelp, but it's not a big problem. Apply some styptic powder to stop the bleeding and keep in mind that you don't want to go that low as you cut the others.

As your Springer grows older and less active, she will need her nails trimmed more often.

Cleaning Ears

English Springer Spaniels have long, soft beautiful ears. However, Springers' ears can cause problems because they restrict the flow of air to the ear canal. This can make ears a problem zone if they are not properly taken care of. Ear-cleaning is something you must learn to do if you are going to have a Springer in your family. It must be part of your regular routine and should be done at least once a week—more often if there are problems or if your veterinarian recommends it.

Lift the ear flap, and gently swab the ear with a cotton ball dampened with witch hazel. Take care not to probe deeply. Every few months, it's also a good idea to trim hair from the inside and outside the ear flap, thus allowing air to circulate more freely. You'll need clippers or scissors for this procedure. Lift the ear flap and snip or buzz the hair off around the upper third of the ear. Do the same thing around the outside of the ear. If you use the clippers, move them against the direction that the hair grows.

If you notice lots of dark wax or a bad smell as you are cleaning, it probably means an ear infection. Other signs of an ear infection include your dog shaking his

GROOMING TOOLS

pin brush

slicker brush

flea comb

towel

mat rake

grooming glove

scissors

nail clippers

tooth-cleaning equipment

shampoo

conditioner

clippers

63

head, pawing at his ear or inclining his head to one side. Take your dog to the vet, who will probably prescribe ear drops to clear up the infection.

Attending to Feet

Besides nail care, the feet need other attention. The hair on the feet needs to be trimmed regularly so it doesn't catch sharp things. To trim the hair on the pads, lift up the foot and cut the hair even with the pads. To trim the hair on the top of the foot, hold the foot firmly and trim the hair level with the bottom of the pad. To trim between the toes, raise hairs against the grain and cut downwards. This will keep the Springer's step in fine form and will prevent nasty thing from getting caught in his hair and injuring his feet.

Trimming around your dog's feet will keep them from picking up thorns or other harmful objects.

Bathing Your Dog

A dog who is brushed daily should not have to be bathed often, unless he gets muddy or rolls in something smelly, which is bound to happen at some point!

When a bath is necessary, make sure you have everything you need within arm's reach; if you have to let go of the dog to go get the shampoo, I assure you he will not be there when you return! Also, dress in something that you don't mind getting wet, because you will.

Place a rubber mat on the floor of the tub so that he won't slip. The water should be warm but not hot. The more you do to make the bathing experience pleasant for your dog, the easier it will be on you. Talk to him gently and massage him as you shampoo.

This dog has been groomed to perfection for one of the most important days of his life—the Westminster Kennel Club show.

Keep water away from his eyes and *especially* his ears. Water makes the ear a perfect place for bacteria to grow and exacerbates his ear problems. Avoid it at all costs. Consider asking your vet for a drying agent you can apply if water gets in his ears while bathing or swimming.

Rinse him thoroughly in warm water until it runs clear. As he gets out of the tub he will shake all over you and everything else. Throwing a towel over his back might help, but he'll probably just shake it off. When he's done shaking, dry him thoroughly with as many towels as it takes. Then brush and comb his coat. You can use a blow dryer to speed the drying process. Of course, if it's cold outside, don't let him out until he's thoroughly dry (except to relieve himself), and you may find the hair dryer useful in this case. If you do use it, make sure you keep it on a low setting.

Trimming

Show Springers are trimmed along the legs, body, and feet for a sleeker, well-coiffured look. It isn't necessary, but if you want your Springer to look his best, this is an easy way to polish off a nice appearance. You can trim the feathering on the legs and body with a pair of straight scissors to neaten up your Springer's appearance.

Keeping Your
English Springer Spaniel
Healthy

If your English Springer Spaniel is not feeling well, he won't be able to tell you what's wrong; it's up to you to recognize when he's "off," and take proper care of him.

If you take proper regular care of him, including giving him high-quality food and enough exercise, the times when your English Springer Spaniel is really sick should

be infrequent. If you learn to recognize when your Springer's not feeling his best, you can keep minor problems from escalating into major ones.

This chapter begins with preventive care information, then explores common canine health problems and progresses to more serious problems, including diseases your English Springer Spaniel is particularly prone to.

Preventive Care

The easiest way to make sure your dog is well cared for is to establish a routine, then follow it every day.

For optimal health, your English Springer Spaniel needs high-quality dog food (Chapter 5), fresh, clean water, exercise and sleep (Chapter 4). He needs these every day, in varying amounts as he grows older. Beyond this basic care, make sure you give your Springer a good going-over every day. By this I mean you should run your hands over your English Springer Spaniel. As you do this you will get to know the feel of your dog. You can do this while you're grooming him. Run your fingers through and under the coat so you can feel the dog's skin. Should he pick up a tick, you will feel it with your fingers. If he has a cut, a lump or bruise or a skin rash, you will feel it.

By checking the dog like this every day, you will find these things before they turn into bigger problems. When you start this routine in puppyhood, your dog will come to love it and will be more accepting of being petted by other people—especially the veterinarian—as an adult.

Puppies are especially vulnerable to many canine diseases, so be sure to stick to your vaccination schedule.

Going Over Your Dog

The best time for this exam is after you have brushed your English Springer Spaniel. Start at your dog's head and, using your fingertips to navigate through the fur, feel all over your dog's head, including around his muzzle, eyes, ears and neck. Take your time and be gentle.

Continue working your hands down your Springer's body, examining his shoulders, back, sides and legs. Run your hands down each leg, handling each toe on each paw, checking for bumps, burrs, cuts and scratches. If you find any minor cuts and scrapes, wash them off with soap and water and apply a mild antibiotic ointment. However, if a cut is gaping or looks red and inflamed, call your veterinarian. Check your Springer's tummy, too. Fleas like to hide in the groin area and behind elbows—don't miss those spots.

Once you've gone over his entire body this way, return to his head. It's time to check your English Springer Spaniel's mouth, looking for inflamed gums, foreign objects or possible cracked or broken teeth. Become familiar with what the teeth look like, inside and out. This is a good time to brush the teeth, as discussed in Chapter 6.

Next, clean the inside of the ears, gently wiping them with cotton balls moistened with witch hazel or a commercial product made especially for cleaning the ears. As you wipe out the ear, check for scratches or foreign objects, and give the ear a sniff. If there is quite a bit of discharge and the ear has a sour smell, call your veterinarian; your dog may have an ear infection.

Check your Springer's nails. Even though they don't need to be clipped every day, they should be checked for chips or cracks or anything else that may need veterinary attention.

Choosing a Veterinarian

Another excellent preventive care measure you can take with your English Springer Spaniel is to find the right veterinarian for him and for you. Your English Springer Spaniel's veterinarian should be someone who understands the breed and is not intimidated or overly judgmental about it.

Your Springer's veterinarian should be someone with whom you feel comfortable asking questions, who takes the time to explain things to you, who lets you know how emergency or after-hour situations are handled by the office and of whose competence you're assured. If possible, get a recommendation from your puppy's breeder. If that's not possible, ask local veterinarians about their experiences with English Springer Spaniels and interview them over the phone before scheduling a visit.

Tail Docking and Dewclaw Removal

Chances are that by the time you purchase your puppy his tail will have already been docked; it is usually done at three to six days old by a veterinarian. A field Springer will have a slightly longer tail; usually only one-third of the tail is docked. Your veterinarian will want to check to see that the tail is completely healed; it should be.

Front dewclaws—a dog's "fifth toe"—which grow higher up on the dog's leg, are routinely removed at the time of tail docking. Examine your puppy for rear dewclaws, which are present in approximately a quarter of Springers. These should be removed as well or the toenail on this odd toe will grow into the skin and leg, causing the dog great pain.

YOUR PUPPY'S VACCINES

Vaccines are given to prevent your dog from getting an infectious disease like canine distemper or rabies. Vaccines are the ultimate preventive medicine: they're given before your dog ever gets the disease so as to protect him from the disease. That's why it is necessary for your dog to be vaccinated routinely. Puppy vaccines start at eight weeks of age for the five-in-one DHLPP vaccine and are given every three to four weeks until the puppy is sixteen months old. Your veterinarian will put your puppy on a proper schedule and will remind you when to bring in your dog for shots.

Vaccines

These are another aspect of preventive care. If given at the correct ages, vaccines will protect your Springer from some potentially life-threatening infectious diseases. These are diseases caused by bacteria, viruses, protozoa, fungi and rickettsia. Young puppies are especially susceptible. Your English Springer Spaniel may have already received some of his shots before you brought him home. Keep him on the vaccination schedule your breeder and/or veterinarian prescribes.

Infectious diseases include distemper, infectious hepatitis, leptospirosis, parvovirus, coronavirus, parainfluenza (kennel cough) and rabies.

DISTEMPER

Distemper is a very contagious viral disease that used to kill thousands of dogs. Today's vaccines are extremely effective, but dogs still die from it. If your Springer has an immune-system problem, or if he wasn't properly vaccinated as a puppy, he could get distemper. Symptoms show as weakness and depression, a fever and a discharge from the eyes and nose. Infected dogs cough, vomit and have diarrhea. Intravenous fluids and antibiotics may help support an infected dog, but unfortunately, most die.

CANINE HEPATITIS

This is a highly contagious virus that primarily attacks the liver but can also cause severe kidney damage. It is not related to the form of hepatitis that affects people. The virus is spread through contaminated saliva, mucus, urine or feces. Initial symptoms include depression, vomiting, abdominal pain, high fever and jaundice. Mild cases may be treated with intravenous fluids, antibiotics and even blood transfusions; however, the mortality rate is very high.

LEPTOSPIROSIS

Leptospirosis is a bacterial disease spread by the urine of infected wildlife. If your English Springer Spaniel drinks from a contaminated stream or sniffs at a bush that has been urinated on by an infected animal, it may pick up the bacteria. The bacteria attacks the kidneys, causing kidney failure. Symptoms include fever, loss of appetite, possible diarrhea and jaundice. Antibiotics can be used to treat the disease, but the outcome is usually not good, due to the serious kidney and liver damage caused by the bacteria. Leptospirosis is highly contagious; other dogs, animals and people are susceptible.

PARVOVIRUS

Parvovirus, or parvo as it is commonly known, atttacks the inner lining of the intestines, causing bloody diarrhea that has a distinct odor. It is a terrible killer of puppies and is extremely contagious. In puppies under ten weeks of age, the virus also attacks the heart, causing death, often with no other symptoms. The virus moves rapidly and dehydration can lead to shock and death in a matter of hours.

CORONAVIRUS

As is implied by the name, this is also a virus. Coronavirus is rarely fatal to adult dogs, although it is frequently fatal to puppies. The symptoms include vomiting, loss of appetite and a yellowish, watery stool that might contain mucus or blood. The stools carry the shed virus, which is highly contagious.

PARAINFLUENZA (KENNEL COUGH)

This respiratory infection can be caused by any number of different viral or bacterial agents. These highly contagious, airborne agents can cause a variety of symptoms, including inflammation of the trachea, bronchi and lungs, as well as mild to severe coughing. Antibiotics may be prescribed to combat or prevent pneumonia, and a cough suppressant may quiet the cough. Luckily, the disease is usually mild, and many dogs recover quickly without any treatment at all.

ADVANTAGES OF SPAY/NEUTER

The greatest advantage of spaying (for females) or neutering (for males) your dog is that you are guaranteed your dog will not produce puppies. There are too many puppies already available for too few homes. There are other advantages as well.

ADVANTAGES OF SPAYING

No messy heats.

No "suitors" howling at your windows or waiting in your yard.

Decreased incidences of pyometra (disease of the uterus) and breast cancer.

ADVANTAGES OF NEUTERING

Lessens male aggressive and territorial behaviors, but doesn't affect the dog's personality. Behaviors are often owner-induced, so neutering is not the only answer, but it is a good start.

Prevents the need to roam in search of bitches in season.

Decreased incidences of urogenital diseases.

RABIES

Rabies is a highly infectious virus usually carried by wildlife, especially bats, raccoons and skunks. Any warm-blooded animal, including humans, can be infected. The virus is transmitted through the saliva, through a bite or break in the skin. It then travels up to the brain and spinal cord and throughout the body. Behavior changes are the first sign of the disease. Animals usually only seen at night will come out during the day; fearful or shy animals will become bold and aggressive or friendly and affectionate. As the virus spreads, the animal will have trouble swallowing and will drool or salivate excessively. Paralysis and convulsions follow.

There are vaccines to combat all these diseases, and they're most effective when given at the right times and boostered regularly by your veterinarian.

Unfortunately, vaccinations are no guarantee that your English Springer Spaniel will not get sick. Many factors determine how well a dog reacts to a vaccination, including the antibodies he got from his mother, how his own immune system reacts to the vaccine, and the dog's general state of health.

Spaying and Neutering

One of the best preventive medicines you can give your English Springer Spaniel is a spay or neuter operation. The spay operation is for females and removes their uterus, tubes and ovaries. When a male dog is neutered (castrated), his testicles are removed.

The only reason not to spay or neuter your dog is if the puppy is of show quality and you intend to show him or her. If you bought your puppy from a breeder, that person will probably have sold you your dog with a contract. Depending on the breeder's assessment of your puppy, the contract will either obligate you to spay or neuter the dog by a certain age or show the dog by a certain age. If the latter is the case and for some reason the dog cannot or will not be shown, then the breeder and owner can discuss spaying or neutering the dog.

Spaying or neutering your English Springer Spaniel will prevent her or him from reproducing. Many people breed, or want to breed, their dogs for the wrong reasons. One of the most common is that they love their pet and want to have a puppy just like him or her.

Spaying and neutering won't make your pet fat. Plenty of exercise and the right amount of food is the only way to keep your pet fit and trim.

Unfortunately, a puppy from their treasured pet will not be the same. The genetic combination that created their pet was from that pet's ancestors. A puppy will be from that pet *and* from the dog they breed the pet to. If you want a dog very much like the one you have, go back to the breeder where you got your dog and get another from the same lineage.

Many people feel their dog should be allowed to reproduce because it is a purebred or because it has "papers." This, however, is no assurance of quality. If you're not showing or interested in showing, you probably have a pet-quality dog. A wonderful dog, I'm sure, but not one that should necessarily be bred. Discuss this matter with a breeder if you feel strongly about breeding your Springer.

Another reason people give for wanting to breed their dogs is so their children can see the miracle of birth. This "miracle" usually comes late at night or very early in the morning, when the kids are asleep. It can also be a heartbreaking miracle if anything goes wrong, and there is plenty that can go wrong.

The health benefits of spaying and neutering are numerous. Researchers have found that spayed and neutered dogs have less incidence of cancer later in life—up to 90 percent less. That alone is incredible. In addition, the lessened hormone drive in both males and females makes them much better companions.

Spaying and neutering serves other purposes, as well. A male dog that has been neutered (castrated) is less likely to roam, is less likely to show aggression toward other dogs and will be less likely to urinate to mark territory. A female dog in season (receptive to males) will attract hordes of male dogs that wish to breed her. A spayed female dog will not, of course, go through that heat season.

One myth about spaying and neutering is that it will make your pet fat. There is nothing about this procedure that creates obesity. The only thing that does is too much food and not enough exercise. It's up to you to make sure your dog has the right amount of both.

Common Canine Health Problems

This section will cover the ailments to which all dogs are prone: fleas, ticks, worms and so on. If you have specific questions or concerns, consult your veterinarian.

EXTERNAL PARASITES

FLEAS

A flea is a tiny insect about the size of a pin head that lives by biting its host and eating its blood. It is crescent shaped, has six legs and is a tremendous jumper.

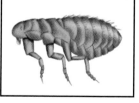

The flea is a die-hard pest.

You'll know your English Springer Spaniel has fleas if, during your daily inspection of his skin, you see a tiny darting speck trying to hide in his fur. Fleas best show up on the dog's belly, near the genitals. If you brush your Springer vigorously and you see little black specks falling to the ground, your dog has fleas. Those specks are "flea dirt," the digested, excreted blood produced by the fleas.

Fleas are extremely annoying because they cause your dog a lot of misery, and they're hard to get rid of. But more than that, they're a serious health hazard. A heavy infestation can actually kill a dog, especially very young and very old dogs. Keep in mind that each time a flea bites, it eats a drop or two of blood. Multiply that by numerous bites a day times the number of fleas, and you can see how dangerous an infestation can be.

Fleas can also cause other problems. Many English Springer Spaniels are allergic to the flea's saliva and scratch each bite until a sore develops. This flea allergy dermatitis is a serious problem in many areas of the country. Fleas can also carry disease, such as the infamous bubonic plague, and are the intermediary host for tapeworms, an internal parasite.

Treating Fleas To reduce the flea population, you need to treat the dog *and its environment,* including inside and outside the house. If you treat only the dog and do not treat the house, yard and car, your English Springer Spaniel will simply become reinfected. Flea eggs can live for years in the right environment, just waiting for the chance to rehatch. That's why it's so important to rid your dog, your home and your car of any possibility of fleas.

There are a number of flea-killing products on the market, including both strong chemical insecticides and natural botanical products. There is also a new medication available you can give your pet once a month that kills fleas after they bite your dog but is not harmful to the dog; ask your veterinarian about it.

What you decide to use depends upon how bad your flea infestation is and your personal preferences.

FIGHTING FLEAS

Remember, the fleas you see on your dog are only part of the problem—the smallest part! To rid your dog and home of fleas, you need to treat your dog *and* your home. Here's how:

• Identify where your pet(s) sleep. These are "hot spots."

• Clean your pets' bedding regularly by vacuuming and washing.

• Spray "hot spots" with a non-toxic, long-lasting flea larvicide.

• Treat outdoor "hot spots" with insecticide.

• Kill eggs on pets with a product containing insect growth regulators (IGRs).

• Kill fleas on pets per your veterinarian's recommendation.

The stronger chemicals, such as organophosphates and carbamates, will kill the fleas, of course, but they can also kill birds and wildlife. You must read the directions and use them properly.

The natural products are not as strong and some do not kill the fleas immediately; sometimes it takes a few hours. Some products use silica or diatomaceous earth to cut or erode the flea's shell so that it dehydrates. There are also commercial products that use natural oils, such as pennyroyal, eucalyptus or citrus to repel the fleas. Use these products according to directions, as even natural products can be harmful when used incorrectly.

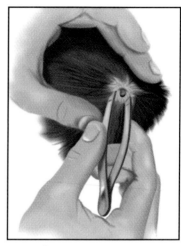

If you have any questions about what is safe to use on your dog, call your veterinarian or groomer. If you have questions as to how to use a particular product, call the manufacturer, who will be more than willing to talk to you and explain exactly how the product should be used.

Use tweezers to remove ticks from your dog.

TICKS

There are several varieties of ticks in the United States, the brown dog tick being the most common. This tick is slightly larger than a sesame seed when not engorged with blood. Ticks, like fleas, live off warm-blooded host animals by sucking their blood. Ticks can carry a number of diseases, including Lyme disease, Rocky Mountain Spotted Fever and a number of others, all of which can be very serious.

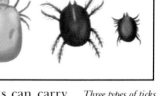

Three types of ticks (l-r): the wood tick, brown dog tick and deer tick.

Check for ticks while you examine your English Springer Spaniel. Ticks seem to prefer to lodge in the ears or in the hair at the base of the ear, the armpits or around the genitals. If you find a tick, smear it thoroughly with petroleum jelly or dab it with hydrogen peroxide, then remove it with tweezers and kill it. Don't try to kill it between your fingers, as it may get blood on you and expose you to the risk of becoming infected or infecting another animal. To kill a tick, put it into a sealed container of alcohol or burn it with a match.

Check your dog for ticks and fleas after she has been outdoors, especially in the spring and summer.

Also, don't just grab and pull or the tick's head may separate from the body. If the head remains in the skin an infection or abscess may result and veterinary treatment may be required. A good method for removing ticks (and fleas) is to spray or dab on a flea or tick-killing product (for use on the animal's skin as opposed to a product for the house or yard), which will kill the pest, making for easy removal. The best way to keep your Springer free from the ills of ticks is to check him every day.

INTERNAL PARASITES

ROUNDWORMS

These long, white worms are a common internal parasite, especially of puppies, although they occasionally infest adult dogs and people. The adult female roundworm can lay up to 200,000 eggs a day, which are passed in the dog's feces. Roundworms are transmitted through the feces of infected animals, so it's important you pick up your own dog's stools daily and prevent your dog from investigating other dogs' feces too closely.

If treated early, roundworms are not serious. However, a heavy infestation can severely affect a dog's health. Puppies with roundworms appear thin, with a dull coat and pot belly. They will not thrive no matter what they eat. In people, roundworms can be more serious; therefore, early treatment, regular fecal checks and good sanitation are important.

HOOKWORMS

Hookworms live their adult lives in the dog's small intestines, where they attach to the intestinal wall and suck blood. When they detach and move to a new location, the old wound continues to bleed because of the anticoagulant the worm injects when it bites. Because of this, bloody diarrhea is usually the first sign of a problem.

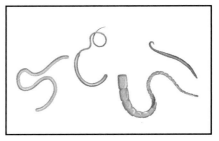

Hookworm eggs, like roundworms, are passed through the feces. They are picked up either from the stools or, if conditions are right, from the soil. This is because the eggs can hatch in the soil, and when a host walks over infested soil, the worms attach themselves to the feet of their new hosts, burrowing into the skin and from there migrating to the intestinal tract, where the cycle starts all over again.

Common internal parasites (l-r): roundworm, whipworm, tapeworm and hookworm.

People, too, can pick up hookworms by walking barefoot in infected soil. In the Sunbelt states, children often pick up hookworm eggs when playing outside in the dirt or in a sandbox. Treatment, for both dogs and people, may have to be repeated.

TAPEWORMS

Tapeworms are also an intestinal feeder, attaching to the intestinal wall to absorb nutrients. They grow by creating new segments. Usually the first sign of an infestation is the rice-like segments found in the stools or on the dog's coat near the rectum. Fleas are the intermediate hosts for tapeworms, and dogs get them when they chew a flea bite and swallow the flea. Therefore, a good flea control program is the best way to prevent a tapeworm infestation.

A FIRST-AID KIT

Keep a canine first-aid kit on hand for general care and emergencies. Check it periodically to make sure liquids haven't spilled or dried up, and replace medications and materials after they're used. Your kit should include:

Activated charcoal tablets

Adhesive tape
(1 and 2 inches wide)

Antibacterial ointment
(for skin and eyes)

Aspirin (buffered or enteric coated, *not* Ibuprofen)

Bandages: Gauze rolls (1 and 2 inches wide) and dressing pads

Cotton balls

Diarrhea medicine

Dosing syringe

Hydrogen peroxide (3%)

Petroleum jelly

Rectal thermometer

Rubber gloves

Rubbing alcohol

Scissors

Tourniquet

Towel

Tweezers

WHIPWORMS

Adult whipworms live in the large intestine, where they feed on blood. The eggs are passed in the stool and can live in the soil for many years. If your dog eats the fresh spring grass, or buries its bone in the yard, it can pick up eggs from the infected soil. If you garden, you can pick up eggs under your fingernails, infecting yourself if you touch your face.

Heavy infestations cause diarrhea, often watery or bloody. The dog may appear thin and anemic, with poor coat. Severe bowel problems may result. Unfortunately, whipworms can be difficult to detect, as the worms do not continually shed eggs. Therefore a stool sample may be clear one day and show eggs the next.

GIARDIA

Giardia is not a worm. It is a protozoan that infects animals through water. Giardia are common to wild animals in many areas, so your English Springer Spaniel can pick it up from drinking from a water source where wild animals are living. That's why it's a good idea to bring water from home if you do any exploring of wild areas with your Springer.

Diarrhea is one of the first symptoms of giardiasis, a giardial infection. If your dog has diarrhea and you and your dog have been out camping, make sure you tell your veterinarian.

HEARTWORM

Pet owners hear a lot about heartworm these days. Heartworm is spread by infected mosquitoes (the intermediate host), which are common to many parts of the country. In most areas, dogs are put on heartworm preventative for most if not all of the year. This is because heartworm is so much easier to prevent than to cure.

Even if your pet can't get out of your yard, wild animals may find a way in. If there's an emergency, know how to contact your veterinarian after-hours.

Adult heartworms live in the upper heart and greater pulmonary arteries, where they severely damage the vessel walls. They are large worms and quickly clog the heart and pulmonary arteries. Poor circulation results, which in turn causes damage to other bodily functions; eventually, death from heart failure results.

Before starting a heartworm preventative, your dog *must* be tested for the presence of heartworm and the results must be negative.

First Aid and Emergencies

Your English Springer Spaniel cannot tell you when he is sick, but if you spend enough time with him and are observant of his behavior, you'll notice when he's feeling off. When you notice anything unusual in the way he's acting, ask yourself these questions:

What caused you to think there was a problem?

What was your first clue there was something wrong?

Is your English Springer Spaniel eating normally?

Does your Springer have a temperature? (Read on for instructions on taking your dog's temperature.)

What do his stools look like?

Is your Springer limping?

When you do a hands-on exam, is he sore anywhere? Can you feel a lump?

Is anything red or swollen?

Run your hands regularly over your dog to feel for any injuries.

Write down anything you've noticed. When you call your veterinarian, be prepared to give specific details about your English Springer Spaniel.

The following are examples of problems that require first aid. The advice is minimal, and is not intended as a substitute for veterinary care. Do what you can to help your dog, then call your veterinarian.

If something happens to your English Springer Spaniel during nonregular veterinary visiting hours, it's important to have an emergency number to call. Ask your veterinarian for this number on your first visit and keep it by the phone. You won't want to be scrambling for it when a real emergency strikes. And you won't want to be struggling with directions in the middle of the night if you've never been to the emergency clinic before. It's a good idea to do a practice run to the emergency clinic during a nonemergency. You'll need all the calm you can muster in a real emergency, and knowing how long it will take to get to the clinic is important.

Taking Your Dog's Temperature

Your vet will ask if your dog has a fever. You can take your dog's temperature using a rectal thermometer (the kind used for people). A dog's normal temperature is between 101 and 102 degrees Fahrenheit. Shake the thermometer down and put some petroleum jelly on it. If possible, ask someone to help you by holding your Springer at his head so he can't squirm around too much. Lift up your Springer's tail and insert the thermometer into the anus about one inch. Don't let go of it! Keep holding the thermometer and watch your clock. After three minutes, withdraw the thermometer, wipe it off and read the temperature.

Vomiting

Your veterinarian will ask if your dog is vomiting. He or she will also ask what the vomit looked like. Is it vomit (digested food) or regurgitated food (which never makes it farther than the esophagus and looks like slime-covered food)? Was there anything unusual in it, like garbage or glass or plant matter? Was it one instance or several?

Unusual Bowel Movements

Similar questions will be asked about the dog's bowel movements. Did the dog have a bowel movement? If so, did it look normal? Was there mucus or blood in the stool? Did the stool have a different or peculiar smell? Did you see any foreign objects in the stool?

Your veterinarian will still want to see your English Springer Spaniel to be sure, but your answers to these questions will help a lot to establish an early diagnosis and to prepare your veterinarian for what to expect when you come in.

DIARRHEA

Diarrhea can be caused by many things, but it all comes out as loose, watery stools. (Severe diarrhea, which is accompanied by straining and blood in the stools, is called colitis.) Basically, diarrhea occurs when your dog eats something she shouldn't, like garbage, spoiled food, another animal's feces, plants, etc. Once the offending matter has passed, the diarrhea goes away. You can help your dog feel better by feeding small meals of a bland diet such as boiled meat and plain rice; making sure there's plenty of water available (diarrhea is extremely dehydrating); giving your dog an anti-diarrheal medicine such as Loperamide. If diarrhea persists or looks particularly bad, consult your veterinarian immediately.

ANIMAL BITES

If your Springer is bitten by another dog or other animal and he's in pain, you'll need to put a temporary muzzle on him. That way you can touch the area of the wound without getting bitten or snapped at. To make the muzzle, use a pair of panty hose or a long piece of gauze, wrap it around the dog's muzzle, cross under the jaw, then pull it around the dog's head, tieing it in the back.

Use a scarf or old hose to make a temporary muzzle, as shown.

Trim the hair from around the wound and liberally pour hydrogen peroxide over it. A hand-held pressure bandage can help stop the bleeding. Stitches may be necessary if the bite is a rip or tear. Your veterinarian may also recommend putting the dog on antibiotics. Make sure the other animal was not rabid. If you can't be sure but you suspect it was, tell your veterinarian immediately.

BEE STINGS

Many dogs are allergic to bee stings. You'll know if yours is, because the sting will start to swell immediately. Waste no time in getting your dog to the vet, who will give him an antihistamine or other treatment.

BLEEDING

Muzzle your dog if he is in pain. Place a gauze pad or a clean cloth over the wound and apply pressure to stop the bleeding. If the wound will require stitches or if the bleeding doesn't stop, call your vet. If the wound is on a leg and continues to bleed, apply a tourniquet but make sure it is loosened for a few minutes every fifteen minutes. Get to your vet as soon as possible.

CHOKING

If your English Springer Spaniel is pawing at his mouth, gagging, coughing or drooling, he may have something caught in his mouth or throat. Open his jaws and shine a flashlight down the throat. If you can see the object, reach in and pull it out, using your

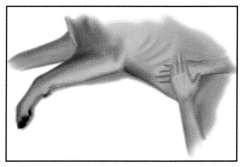

Applying abdominal thrusts can save a choking dog.

fingers, tweezers or a pair of pliers. If you cannot see anything and your dog is still choking, hit the dog behind the neck between the shoulders to try and dislodge the object. If this fails, use an adapted Heimlich maneuver or abdominal thrust.

For the Heimlich maneuver, with your dog standing, grasp either side of the ribcage and squeeze. Don't break ribs, but try to make a sharp enough movement to cause the air in the lungs to force the object out. For the abdominal thrust, lay your dog on his side and, using your palms together, press in quick, sharp motions just behind the ribcage.

If your dog can breathe around the object, get to the vet as soon as possible. If your dog cannot breathe around the object, you don't have time to move the dog. Keep working on getting the object dislodged, while someone takes you and the dog to the vet.

An Elizabethan collar keeps your dog from licking a fresh wound.

FRACTURES

Because your English Springer Spaniel will be in great pain if he has broken a bone, you should muzzle him immediately. Do not try to set the fracture, but try to immobilize the limb in a temporary splint by using a piece of wood and then wrapping it with gauze or soft cloth. If there is a door or board you can use as a backboard or stretcher so the injured limb is stable, do it. Transport the dog to the vet as soon as possible.

Make a temporary splint by wrapping the leg in firm casing, then bandaging it.

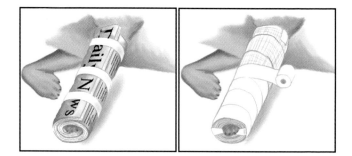

BROKEN NAILS

A ripped or broken toenail can be very painful. If the dog is frantic, muzzle him to protect yourself. If a piece of the nail is hanging, trim it off. Run hydrogen peroxide over the nail. If the nail is bleeding, run it over a soft bar of soap. The soap will help the nail clot. If the quick is showing or if the nail has broken off under the skin, call your veterinarian. Antibiotics might be needed to prevent an infection.

OVERHEATING OR HEAT STROKE

If your Springer is too warm and has difficulty breathing, starts panting rapidly, vomits or collapses, you need to act at once. These are all symptoms of heatstroke, which can be life-threatening. First, check your Springer's tongue. If his usually blue-black tongue shows lighter patches or pink blotches, your diagnosis is confirmed and your dog needs to be cooled *at once.* Immediately place your Springer in a tub of cool water or, if a tub is not available, run water from a hose over your dog. Take his temperature and encourage him to drink some cool water. Call your veterinarian immediately.

POISONING

There is a host of products and plants that can be toxic to your English Springer Spaniel. Antifreeze is one, and dogs are attracted to it because it tastes sweet. Household chemicals, insecticides, paints and various plants are all dangerous to inquiring mouths, which puppies certainly have!

Symptoms of poisoning include retching and vomiting, diarrhea, salivation, labored breathing, dilated pupils, weakness, collapse or convulsions. Sometimes one or more symptoms will appear, depending upon the poison. If you suspect your dog has been in contact with a poison, time is critical. Call your veterinarian right away. If your vet is not immediately available, call the National Animal Poison Control Center hotline (1-800-548-2423). The hotline and your vet can better treat your dog if you can tell them what was ingested and approximately how much. *Do not make your dog vomit unless instructed to do so.*

Some of the many household substances harmful to your dog.

Giving Your Springer Medicine

Some medicines are easy to administer, some are not. Some dogs will take pills or let you put ointment in their eyes easily, some will not. Ask your veterinarian for help, and follow these instructions.

*Squeeze eye oint-
ment into the
lower lid.*

To put eye ointment in the eye without poking the dog with the tube, stand behind your dog and cuddle his head up against your legs. With one hand, gently pull the lower eyelid away from the eye just slightly. At the same time, squeeze some of the ointment into the lower eyelid. When the dog closes his eye, the medication will be distributed over the eye.

There are a couple of different ways to give your dog a pill. The easiest way is to keep a jar of baby food on hand. Dip the pill in it and your Springer should read-

*To give a pill,
open the mouth
wide, then drop
it in the back of
the throat.*

ily lick the pill (with baby food) right from your hand. For those who lick up the food and spit out the pill, you'll need to be more careful. Have your Springer sit and stand behind him, straddling his back. With the pill in one hand, pull your dog's head up and back gently so his muzzle is pointing up. Open his mouth and very quickly drop the pill in the back of his throat. Close his mouth and massage his throat until he swallows. Before you let him go, open his mouth and check to see the pill's gone. Follow up with a treat.

You can give liquid medication the same way, pouring it into your dog's mouth. Be careful that your Springer doesn't inhale the medication instead of swallow it. An easier way is to measure the medicine into a chicken or turkey baster or a large eyedropper, put the tip of the baster into the dog's mouth from the side (between the molars) and, holding the dog's mouth shut, squeeze the medication in while you tilt his head backwards slightly so the medicine runs into instead of out of the mouth.

Applying skin ointments is usually very easy—just part the hair so you're putting the ointment directly on the skin and rub it in according to directions. Keeping your Springer from licking the ointments off can be more difficult, and licking often makes matters worse.

If your dog has a bad skin condition or stitches that need to heal, your veterinarian will probably give you an Elizabethan collar for him. Named for the fashion styles of the reign of Queen Elizabeth I, this is a large plastic collar that extends at least to the tip of your dog's nose. The collar is ugly and clumsy, and most dogs absolutely hate it, but it's the only thing that will give the wound a good chance to heal.

Remember, whenever your veterinarian prescribes a treatment or medication, don't be afraid to ask questions. Ask what the drug(s) is, what it does and how long your dog should take it. Ask if there are any side effects you should watch for. Make sure you understand what your dog's problem is, what the course of treatment will do and what you should (or should not) expect. That done, make sure you follow through on the course of treatment. If your veterinarian said to give the medication for ten days, give it for ten days. Don't stop at five days just because your dog looks better. Again, if you have any problems or reservations, call your vet.

Check your dog's teeth frequently and brush them regularly.

Problems Particular to the English Springer Spaniel

EAR INFECTIONS

As we've mentioned before, the Springer's long ears mean more ear trouble than in breeds with ears that stand upright. See Chapter 6, "Grooming Your English Springer Spaniel," for complete information on ear cleaning. See your veterinarian if you suspect something is amiss. Extended ear infections can cause partial or total deafness, so don't delay treatment.

CANINE HIP DYSPLASIA

Hip dysplasia is a developmental abnormality of the hip joints caused by laxity within the joint. Changes in bone size, shape and structure occur as the hips attempt to compensate for abnormal stresses on the joints. Dogs with hip dysplasia may exhibit lameness at some time in their life. By the time affected dogs are two years of age, hip dysplasia is detectable by X-raying the hips. Older dogs (eighteen months to ten years) with hip dysplasia may have a slow onset of painful arthritis in the hips.

HEREDITARY EYE DISEASES

The eyes of English Springer Spaniels are susceptible to several genetic-based disorders, some of which are present at birth and others that may develop at various times throughout life.

Retinal dysplasia is a developmental malformation of the retina. Affected puppies are born with the disorder. Most cases of retinal dysplasia are mild. Small areas of retinal degeneration occur on the surface of the retina, with no detectable loss in vision. These abnormalities are detectable by veterinary ophthalmologists when puppies are seven to twelve weeks old. Retinal dysplasia should not affect a dog's ability to function as a pet.

Progressive Retinal Atrophy (PRA) is a degeneration of the layers of the retina that are responsible for vision. The disease is progressive, eventually resulting in blindness. The onset of PRA in English Springer Spaniels is variable, but usually occurs between two and six years of age. Although the disorder is rare in English Springer Spaniels, its incidence has increased some in the last few years. There is no pain or discomfort with PRA, but unfortunately, there is no treatment.

Eyelid defects occasionally occur in English Springer Spaniels. Entropion is an inward folding of the lower eyelid that results in chronic irritation of the surface of the eye. It is usually observed within the first year of life. Entropion is treated by surgically eliminating the defect.

AGGRESSIVE TEMPERAMENT

Temperament and behavior problems happen in all breeds of dogs. Behavior is influenced by many factors, not only genetics, but training, family interactions, health and so on. Sometimes aggressive temperament is incorrectly called "rage syndrome" in Springers. True rage syndrome is rare and is thought to be caused by a condition similar to epilepsy. But, instead of seizuring, the dog will attack his owner or someone else without provocation. Afterwards, the dog seems confused and unaware of what has just happened.

SEIZURE DISORDERS

Hereditary seizures are relatively rare in English Springer Spaniels. Some cases of seizures in Springers are not controlled with treatment. Seizures usually begin before the age of five years. In many cases, seizures can be controlled with medication.

Fortunately, English Springers seem to be relatively free of the hereditary ailments that plague some breeds. If you keep your Springer in good physical health with good quality food, plenty of exercise and regular grooming, he should live a long and healthy life.

As Your English Springer Spaniel Ages

English Springer Spaniels can, on the average, live twelve to fourteen years. However, to live that long in good health, your English Springer Spaniel will need your help. Aging in dogs, as in people, brings some changes and problems. Your Springer's vision will dim, his hearing fade and his joints stiffen. Heart and kidney disease are common in older dogs. Reflexes will not be as sharp as they once were, and your dog may be more sensitive to heat and cold. Your dog may also get grouchy, showing less tolerance to younger dogs, children and other things that may not be part of his normal routine.

Arthritis Arthritis is common in old dogs. The joints get stiff, especially when it's chilly. Your English Springer Spaniel may have trouble getting up in the morning. Make sure he has something soft and warm to sleep on, not just at night, but all day. Talk to your veterinarian about treatment; there are pain relievers that can help.

Nutrition As your dog's activity level slows down, he will need to consume less calories and, as his body ages, he will need less protein. However, some old dogs have a problem digesting foods, too, and this may show up in poor stools and a dull coat. Several dog food manufacturers offer premium quality foods for senior dogs; these foods are more easily digested by the older dog.

Exercise Exercise is still important to your old Springer, who needs the stimulation of walking around and seeing and smelling the world. A leisurely walk around the neighborhood might be enough.

When It's Time There will come a time when you know your dog is suffering more than he needs to, and you will have to decide how to put him out of his pain. Only you can make the decision, but spare your companion the humiliation of incontinence, convulsions or the inability to stand up or move around. Your veterinarian can advise you on the condition of your dog, but don't let him or her make this decision for you.

When you know it's time, call your veterinarian. He or she can give your dog a tranquilizer, then an injection that is an overdose of anesthetic. Your already sleepy dog will quietly stop breathing. Be there with your dog. Let your arms hold your old friend, and let your dog hear your voice saying how much you love him as he goes to sleep. There will be no fear, and the last thing your dog will remember is your love.

Grieving A well-loved dog is an emotional investment of unparalleled returns. Unfortunately, our dogs' lives are entirely too short, and we must learn to cope with inevitably losing them. Grief is a natural reaction to the loss of a loved one, whether it is a pet, a spouse, friend or family member. Grief has no set pattern; its intensity and duration are different for each person and for each loss.

Sometimes the best outlet for grief is a good hard cry. For others, talking about their pet is good therapy. It's especially helpful to talk to people who've also lost an old dog and

IDENTIFYING YOUR DOG

It's a terrible thing to think about, but your dog could somehow, someday, get lost or stolen. How would you get him back? Your best bet would be to have some form of identification on your dog. You can choose from a collar and tags, a tattoo, a microchip or a combination of these three.

Every dog should wear a buckle collar with identification tags. They are the quickest and easiest way for a stranger to identify your dog. It's best to inscribe the tags with your name and phone number; you don't need to include your dog's name.

There are two ways to permanently identify your dog. The first is a tattoo, placed on the inside of your dog's thigh. The tattoo should be your social security number or your dog's AKC registration number.

The second is a microchip, a rice-sized pellet that's inserted under the dog's skin at the base of the neck, between the shoulder blades. When a scanner is passed over the dog, it will beep, notifying the person that the dog has a chip. The scanner will then show a code, identifying the dog. Microchips are becoming more and more popular and are certainly the wave of the future.

can relate to your loss. You may want to bury your old friend in a special spot where you can go to remember the wonderful times you shared together. You could also ask your veterinarian about having your dog cremated and keeping his or her ashes in a special urn in your home.

Your Happy, Healthy Pet

Your Dog's Name _____

Name on Your Dog's Pedigree (if your dog has one) _____

_____

Where Your Dog Came From _____

_____

Your Dog's Birthday _____

Your Dog's Veterinarian

    Name _____

    Address _____

    Phone Number_____

    Emergency Number_____

Your Dog's Health

    Vaccines

    type _____ date given _____

    type _____ date given _____

    type _____ date given _____

    type _____ date given _____

    Heartworm

    date tested _____ type used_____ start date _____

Your Dog's License Number_____

Groomer's Name and Number _____

Dogsitter/Walker's Name and Number_____

Awards Your Dog Has Won

    Award _____ date earned _____

    Award _____ date earned _____

part three

Enjoying
your
Dog

chapter 8

Basic
Training

by Ian Dunbar, Ph.D., MRCVS

Training is the jewel in the crown—the most important aspect of doggy husbandry. There is no more important variable influencing dog behavior and temperament than the dog's education: A well-trained, well-behaved and good-natured puppydog is always a joy to live with, but an untrained and uncivilized dog can be a perpetual nightmare. Moreover, deny the dog an education and she will not have the opportunity to fulfill her own canine potential; neither will she have the ability to communicate effectively with her human companions.

Luckily, modern psychological training methods are easy, efficient, effective and, above all, considerably dog-friendly and user-friendly.

Doggy education is as simple as it is enjoyable. But before you can have a good time play-training with your new dog, you have to learn what to do and how to do it. There is no bigger variable influencing the success of dog training than the *owner's* experience and expertise. *Before you embark on the dog's education, you must first educate yourself.*

Basic Training for Owners

Ideally, basic owner training should begin well *before* you select your dog. Find out all you can about your chosen breed first, then master rudimentary training and handling skills. If you already have your puppy-dog, owner training is a dire emergency—the clock is ticking! Especially for puppies, the first few weeks at home are the most important and influential days in the dog's life. Indeed, the cause of most adolescent and adult problems may be traced back to the initial days the pup explores her new home. This is the time to establish the *status quo*—to teach the puppydog how you would like her to behave and so prevent otherwise quite predictable problems.

In addition to consulting breeders and breed books such as this one (which understandably have a positive breed bias), seek out as many pet owners with your breed as you can find. Good points are obvious. What you want to find out are the breed-specific *problems*, so you can nip them in the bud. In particular, you should talk to owners with *adolescent* dogs and make a list of all anticipated problems. Most important, *test drive* at least half a dozen adolescent and adult dogs of your breed yourself. An 8-week-old puppy is deceptively easy to handle, but she will acquire adult size, speed and strength in just four months, so you should learn now what to prepare for.

Puppy and pet dog training classes offer a convenient venue to locate pet owners and observe dogs in action. For a list of suitable trainers in your area, contact the Association of Pet Dog Trainers (see chapter 13). You may also begin your basic owner training by observing other owners in class. Watch as many classes and test drive as many dogs as possible. Select an upbeat, dog-friendly, people-friendly, fun-and-games, puppydog pet training class to learn the ropes. Also, watch training videos and read training books. You must find out what to do and how to do it *before* you have to do it.

Principles of Training

Most people think training comprises teaching the dog to do things such as sit, speak and roll over, but even a 4-week-old pup knows how to do these things already. Instead, the first step in training involves teaching the dog human words for each dog behavior and activity and for each aspect of the dog's environment. That way you, the owner, can more easily participate in the dog's domestic education by directing her to perform specific actions appropriately, that is, at the right time, in the right place and so on. Training opens communication channels, enabling an educated dog to at least understand her owner's requests.

In addition to teaching a dog *what* we want her to do, it is also necessary to teach her *why* she should do what we ask. Indeed, 95 percent of training revolves around motivating the dog *to want to do* what we want. Dogs often understand what their owners want; they just don't see the point of doing it—especially when the owner's repetitively boring and seemingly senseless instructions are totally at odds with much more pressing and exciting doggy distractions. It is not so much the dog that is being stubborn or dominant; rather, it is the owner who has failed to acknowledge the dog's needs and feelings and to approach training from the dog's point of view.

THE MEANING OF INSTRUCTIONS

The secret to successful training is learning how to use training lures to predict or prompt specific behaviors— to coax the dog to do what you want *when* you want. Any highly valued object (such as a treat or toy) may be used as a lure, which the dog will follow with her eyes and nose. Moving the lure in specific ways entices the dog to move her nose, head and entire body in specific ways. In fact, by learning the art of manipulating various lures, it is possible to teach the dog to assume virtually any body position and perform any action. Once you have control over the expression of the dog's behaviors and can elicit any body position or behavior at will, you can easily teach the dog to perform on request.

Tell your dog what you want her to do, use a lure to entice her to respond correctly, then profusely praise and maybe reward her once she performs the desired action. For example, verbally request "Tina, sit!" while you move a squeaky toy upwards and backwards over the dog's muzzle (lure-movement and hand signal), smile knowingly as she looks up (to follow the lure) and sits down (as a result of canine anatomical engineering), then praise her to distraction ("Gooood Tina!"). Squeak the toy, offer a training treat and give your dog and yourself a pat on the back.

Being able to elicit desired responses over and over enables the owner to reward the dog over and over. Consequently, the dog begins to think training is fun. For example, the more the dog is rewarded for sitting, the more she enjoys sitting. Eventually the dog comes to realize that, whereas most sitting is appreciated, sitting immediately upon request usually prompts especially enthusiastic praise and a slew of high-level rewards. The dog begins to sit on cue much of the time, showing that she is starting to grasp the meaning of the owner's verbal request and hand signal.

WHY COMPLY?

Most dogs enjoy initial lure-reward training and are only too happy to comply with their owners' wishes. Unfortunately, repetitive drilling without appreciative feedback tends to diminish the dog's enthusiasm until she eventually fails to see the point of complying anymore. Moreover, as the dog approaches adolescence she becomes more easily distracted as she develops other interests. Lengthy sessions with repetitive exercises tend to bore and demotivate both parties. If it's not fun, the owner doesn't do it and neither does the dog.

Integrate training into your dog's life: The greater number of training sessions each day and the *shorter* they are, the more willingly compliant your dog will

become. Make sure to have a short (just a few seconds) training interlude before every enjoyable canine activity. For example, ask your dog to sit to greet people, to sit before you throw her Frisbee and to sit for her supper. Really, sitting is no different from a canine "Please."

To train your dog, you need gentle hands, a loving heart and a good attitude.

Also, include numerous short training interludes during every enjoyable canine pastime, for example, when playing with the dog or when she is running in the park. In this fashion, doggy distractions may be effectively converted into rewards for training. Just as all games have rules, fun becomes training . . . and training becomes fun.

Eventually, rewards actually become unnecessary to continue motivating your dog. If trained with consideration and kindness, performing the desired behaviors will become self-rewarding and, in a sense, your dog will motivate herself. Just as it is not necessary to reward a human companion during an enjoyable walk in the park, or following a game of tennis, it is hardly necessary to reward our best friend—the dog—for walking by our side or while playing fetch. Human company during enjoyable activities is reward enough for most dogs.

Even though your dog has become self-motivating, it's still good to praise and pet her a lot and offer rewards once in a while, especially for a good job well done. And if for no other reason, praising and rewarding others is good for the human heart.

PUNISHMENT

Without a doubt, lure-reward training is by far the best way to teach: Entice your dog to do what you want and then reward her for doing so. Unfortunately, a human shortcoming is to take the good for granted and to moan and groan at the bad. Specifically, the dog's many good behaviors are ignored while the owner focuses on punishing the dog for making mistakes. In extreme cases, instruction is *limited* to punishing mistakes made by a trainee dog, child, employee or husband, even though it has been proven punishment training is notoriously inefficient and ineffective and is decidedly unfriendly and combative. It teaches the dog that training is a drag, almost as quickly as it teaches the dog to dislike her trainer. Why treat our best friends like our worst enemies?

Punishment training is also much more laborious and time consuming. Whereas it takes only a finite amount of time to teach a dog what to chew, for example, it takes much, much longer to punish the dog for each and every mistake. Remember, *there is only one right way!* So why not teach that right way from the outset?!

To make matters worse, punishment training causes severe lapses in the dog's reliability. Since it is obviously impossible to punish the dog each and every time she misbehaves, the dog quickly learns to distinguish between those times when she must comply (so as to avoid impending punishment) and those times when she need not comply, because punishment is impossible. Such times include when the dog is off leash and 6 feet away, when the owner is otherwise engaged (talking to a friend, watching television, taking a shower, tending to the baby or chatting on the telephone) or when the dog is left at home alone.

Instances of misbehavior will be numerous when the owner is away, because even when the dog complied in the owner's looming presence, she did so unwillingly. The dog was forced to act against her will, rather than molding her will to want to please. Hence, when the owner is absent, not only does the dog know she need not comply, she simply does not want to. Again, the trainee is not a stubborn vindictive beast, but rather the trainer has failed to teach. Punishment training invariably creates unpredictable Jekyll and Hyde behavior.

Trainer's Tools

Many training books extol the virtues of a vast array of training paraphernalia and electronic and metallic gizmos, most of which are designed for canine restraint, correction and punishment, rather than for actual facilitation of doggy education. In reality, most effective training tools are not found in stores; they come from within ourselves. In addition to a willing dog, all you really need is a functional human brain, gentle hands, a loving heart and a good attitude.

In terms of equipment, all dogs do require a quality buckle collar to sport dog tags and to attach the leash (for safety and to comply with local leash laws). Hollow chew toys (like Kongs or sterilized longbones) and a dog bed or collapsible crate are musts for housetraining. Three additional tools are required:

1. specific lures (training treats and toys) to predict and prompt specific desired behaviors;

2. rewards (praise, affection, training treats and toys) to reinforce for the dog what a lot of fun it all is; and

3. knowledge—how to convert the dog's favorite activities and games (potential distractions to training) into "life-rewards," which may be employed to facilitate training.

The most powerful of these is *knowledge*. Education is the key! Watch training classes, participate in training classes, watch videos, read books, enjoy play-training with your dog and then your dog will say "Please," and your dog will say "Thank you!"

Housetraining

If dogs were left to their own devices, certainly they would chew, dig and bark for entertainment and then no doubt highlight a few areas of their living space with sprinkles of urine, in much the same way we decorate by hanging pictures. Consequently, when we ask a dog to live with us, we must teach her *where* she may dig, *where* she may perform her toilet duties, *what* she may chew and *when* she may bark. After all, when left at home alone for many hours, we cannot expect the dog to amuse herself by completing crosswords or watching the soaps on TV!

Also, it would be decidedly unfair to keep the house rules a secret from the dog, and then get angry and punish the poor critter for inevitably transgressing rules she did not even know existed. Remember: Without adequate education and guidance, the dog will be forced to establish her own rules—doggy rules—and most probably will be at odds with the owner's view of domestic living.

Since most problems develop during the first few days the dog is at home, prospective dog owners must be certain they are quite clear about the principles of housetraining *before* they get a dog. Early misbehaviors quickly become established as the *status quo*—

becoming firmly entrenched as hard-to-break bad habits, which set the precedent for years to come. Make sure to teach your dog good habits right from the start. Good habits are just as hard to break as bad ones!

Ideally, when a new dog comes home, try to arrange for someone to be present as much as possible during the first few days (for adult dogs) or weeks for puppies. With only a little forethought, it is surprisingly easy to find a puppy sitter, such as a retired person, who would be willing to eat from your refrigerator and watch your television while keeping an eye on the newcomer to encourage the dog to play with chew toys and to ensure she goes outside on a regular basis.

POTTY TRAINING

To teach the dog where to relieve herself:

1. never let her make a single mistake;
2. let her know where you want her to go; and
3. handsomely reward her for doing so: "GOOOOOOOD DOG!!!" liver treat, liver treat, liver treat!

Preventing Mistakes

A single mistake is a training disaster, since it heralds many more in future weeks. And each time the dog soils the house, this further reinforces the dog's unfortunate preference for an indoor, carpeted toilet. *Do not let an unhousetrained dog have full run of the house.*

When you are away from home, or cannot pay full attention, confine the dog to an area where elimination is appropriate, such as an outdoor run or, better still, a small, comfortable indoor kennel with access to an outdoor run. When confined in this manner, most dogs will naturally housetrain themselves.

If that's not possible, confine the dog to an area, such as a utility room, kitchen, basement or garage, where elimination may not be desired in the long run but as an interim measure it is certainly preferable to doing it all around the house. Use newspaper to cover the floor of the dog's day room. The newspaper may be used to soak up the urine and to wrap up and dispose of the feces. Once your dog develops a preferred spot for eliminating, it is only necessary to cover

that part of the floor with newspaper. The smaller papered area may then be moved (only a little each day) towards the door to the outside. Thus the dog will develop the tendency to go to the door when she needs to relieve herself.

Never confine an unhousetrained dog to a crate for long periods. Doing so would force the dog to soil the crate and ruin its usefulness as an aid for housetraining (see the following discussion).

Teaching Where

In order to teach your dog where you would like her to do her business, you have to be there to direct the proceedings—an obvious, yet often neglected, fact of life. In order to be there

to teach the dog *where* to go, you need to know *when* she needs to go. Indeed, the success of housetraining depends on the owner's ability to predict these times. Certainly, a regular feeding schedule will facilitate prediction somewhat, but there is nothing like "loading the deck" and influencing the timing of the outcome yourself!

Whenever you are at home, make sure the dog is under constant supervision and/or confined to a small

The first few weeks at home are the most important and influential in your dog's life.

area. If already well trained, simply instruct the dog to lie down in her bed or basket. Alternatively, confine the dog to a crate (doggy den) or tie-down (a short, 18-inch lead that can be clipped to an eye hook in the baseboard near her bed). Short-term close confinement strongly inhibits urination and defecation, since the dog does not want to soil her sleeping area. Thus, when you release the puppydog each hour, she will definitely need to urinate immediately and defecate every third or fourth hour. Keep the dog confined to her doggy den and take her to her intended toilet area each hour, every hour and on the hour.

When taking your dog outside, instruct her to sit quietly before opening the door—she will soon learn to sit by the door when she needs to go out!

Teaching Why

Being able to predict when the dog needs to go enables the owner to be on the spot to praise and reward the dog. Each hour, hurry the dog to the intended toilet area in the yard, issue the appropriate instruction ("Go pee!" or "Go poop!"), then give the dog three to four minutes to produce. Praise and offer a couple of training treats when successful. The treats are important because many people fail to praise their dogs with feeling . . . and housetraining is hardly the time for understatement. So either loosen up and enthusiastically praise that dog: "Wuzzzer-wuzzer-wuzzer, hoooser good wuffer den? Hoooo went pee for Daddy?" Or say "Good dog!" as best you can and offer the treats for effect.

Following elimination is an ideal time for a spot of play-training in the yard or house. Also, an empty dog may be allowed greater freedom around the house for the next half hour or so, just as long as you keep an eye out to make sure she does not get into other kinds of mischief. If you are preoccupied and cannot pay full attention, confine the dog to her doggy den once more to enjoy a peaceful snooze or to play with her many chew toys.

If your dog does not eliminate within the allotted time outside—no biggie! Back to her doggy den, and then try again after another hour.

As I own large dogs, I always feel more relaxed walking an empty dog, knowing that I will not need to finish our stroll weighted down with bags of feces!

Beware of falling into the trap of walking the dog to get her to eliminate. The good ol' dog walk is such an enormous highlight in the dog's life that it represents the single biggest potential reward in domestic dogdom. However, when in a hurry, or during inclement weather, many owners abruptly terminate the walk the moment the dog has done her business. This, in effect, severely punishes the dog for doing the right thing, in the right place at the right time. Consequently, many dogs become strongly inhibited from eliminating outdoors because they know it will signal an abrupt end to an otherwise thoroughly enjoyable walk.

Instead, instruct the dog to relieve herself in the yard prior to going for a walk. If you follow the above instructions, most dogs soon learn to eliminate on cue. As soon as the dog eliminates, praise (and offer a treat or two)—"Good dog! Let's go walkies!" Use the walk as a reward for eliminating in the yard. If the dog does not go, put her back in her doggy den and think about a walk later on. You will find with a "No feces—no walk" policy, your dog will become one of the fastest defecators in the business.

If you do not have a backyard, instruct the dog to eliminate right outside your front door prior to the walk. Not only will this facilitate clean up and disposal of the feces in your own trash can but, also, the walk may again be used as a colossal reward.

CHEWING AND BARKING

Short-term close confinement also teaches the dog that occasional quiet moments are a reality of domestic living. Your puppydog is extremely impressionable during her first few weeks at home. Regular

confinement at this time soon exerts a calming influence over the dog's personality. Remember, once the
dog is housetrained and calmer, there will be a whole
lifetime ahead for the dog to enjoy full run of the
house and garden. On the other hand, by letting the
newcomer have unrestricted access to the entire household and allowing her to run willy-nilly, she will most
certainly develop a bunch of behavior problems in
short order, no doubt necessitating confinement later
in life. It would not be fair to remedially restrain and
confine a dog you have trained, through neglect, to
run free.

When confining the dog, make sure she always has an
impressive array of suitable chew toys. Kongs and sterilized longbones (both readily available from pet
stores) make the best chew toys, since they are hollow
and may be stuffed with treats to heighten the dog's
interest. For example, by stuffing the little hole at the
top of a Kong with a small piece of freeze-dried liver,
the dog will not want to leave it alone.

Remember, treats do not have to be junk food and
they certainly should not represent extra calories.
Rather, treats should be part of each dog's regular

daily diet: Some food
may be served in the
dog's bowl for break-
fast and dinner, some
food may be used as
training treats, and
some food may be
used for stuffing chew
toys. I regularly stuff
my dogs' many Kongs
with different shaped
biscuits and kibble.

*Make sure your
puppy has suit-
able chew toys.*

The kibble seems to fall out fairly easily, as do the
oval-shaped biscuits, thus rewarding the dog instanta-
neously for checking out the chew toys. The bone-
shaped biscuits fall out after a while, rewarding the dog
for worrying at the chew toy. But the triangular biscuits
never come out. They remain inside the Kong as lures,

maintaining the dog's fascination with her chew toy. To further focus the dog's interest, I always make sure to flavor the triangular biscuits by rubbing them with a little cheese or freeze-dried liver.

To teach come, call your dog, open your arms as a welcoming signal, wave a toy or a treat and praise for every step in your direction.

If stuffed chew toys are reserved especially for times the dog is confined, the puppydog will soon learn to enjoy quiet moments in her doggy den and she will quickly develop a chew-toy habit— a good habit! This is a simple *autoshaping* process; all the owner has to do is set up the situation and the dog all but trains herself— easy and effective. Even when the dog is given run of the house, her first inclination will be to indulge her rewarding chew-toy habit rather than destroy less-attractive household articles, such as curtains, carpets, chairs and compact disks. Similarly, a chew-toy chewer will be less inclined to scratch and chew herself excessively. Also, if the dog busies herself as a recreational chewer, she will be less inclined to develop into a recreational barker or digger when left at home alone.

Stuff a number of chew toys whenever the dog is left confined and remove the extra-special-tasting treats when you return. Your dog will now amuse herself with her chew toys before falling asleep and then resume playing with her chew toys when she expects you to return. Since most owner-absent misbehavior happens right after you leave and right before your expected return, your puppydog will now be conveniently preoccupied with her chew toys at these times.

Come and Sit

Most puppies will happily approach virtually anyone, whether called or not; that is, until they collide with adolescence and develop other more important doggy interests, such as sniffing a multiplicity of exquisite odors on the grass. Your mission, Mr./Ms. Owner, is to teach and reward the pup for coming reliably, willingly and happily when called—and you have just three months to get it done. Unless adequately reinforced, your puppy's tendency to approach people will self-destruct by adolescence.

Call your dog ("Tina, come!"), open your arms (and maybe squat down) as a welcoming signal, waggle a treat or toy as a lure and reward the puppydog when she comes running. Do not wait to praise the dog until she reaches you—she may come 95 percent of the way and then run off after some distraction. Instead, praise the dog's *first* step towards you and continue praising enthusiastically for *every* step she takes in your direction.

When the rapidly approaching puppy dog is three lengths away from impact, instruct her to sit ("Tina, sit!") and hold the lure in front of you in an outstretched hand to prevent her from hitting you midchest and knocking you flat on your back! As Tina decelerates to nose the lure, move the treat upwards and backwards just over her muzzle with an upwards motion of your extended arm (palm-upwards). As the dog looks up to follow the lure, she will sit down (if she jumps up, you are holding the lure too high). Praise the dog for sitting. Move backwards and call her again. Repeat this many times over, always praising when Tina comes and sits; on occasion, reward her.

For the first couple of trials, use a training treat both as a lure to entice the dog to come and sit and as a reward for doing so. Thereafter, try to use different items as lures and rewards. For example, lure the dog with a Kong or Frisbee but reward her with a food treat. Or lure the dog with a food treat but pat her and throw a tennis ball as a reward. After just a few repetitions, dispense with the lures and rewards; the dog will begin to respond willingly to your verbal requests and hand signals just for the prospect of praise from your heart and affection from your hands.

Instruct every family member, friend and visitor how to get the dog to come and sit. Invite people over for a series of pooch parties; do not keep the pup a secret— let other people enjoy this puppy, and let the pup enjoy other people. Puppydog parties are not only fun, they easily attract a lot of people to help *you* train *your* dog. Unless you teach your dog how to meet people, that is, to sit for greetings, no doubt the dog will resort to jumping up. Then you and the visitors will get annoyed, and the dog will be punished. This is not fair. *Send out those invitations for puppy parties and teach your dog to be mannerly and socially acceptable.*

Even though your dog quickly masters obedient recalls in the house, her reliability may falter when playing in the backyard or local park. Ironically, it is *the owner* who has unintentionally trained the dog *not* to respond in these instances. By allowing the dog to play and run around and otherwise have a good time, but then to call the dog to put her on leash to take her home, the dog quickly learns playing is fun but training is a drag. Thus, playing in the park becomes a severe distraction, which works against training. Bad news!

Instead, whether playing with the dog off leash or on leash, request her to come at frequent intervals—say, every minute or so. On most occasions, praise and pet the dog for a few seconds while she is sitting, then tell her to go play again. For especially fast recalls, offer a couple of training treats and take the time to praise and pet the dog enthusiastically before releasing her. The dog will learn that coming when called is not necessarily the end of the play session, and neither is it the end of the world; rather, it signals an enjoyable, quality time-out with the owner before resuming play once more. In fact, playing in the park now becomes a very effective life-reward, which works to facilitate training by reinforcing each obedient and timely recall. Good news!

Sit, Down, Stand and Rollover

Teaching the dog a variety of body positions is easy for owner and dog, impressive for spectators and extremely useful for all. Using lure-reward techniques, it is possible to train several positions at once to verbal commands or hand signals (which impress the socks off onlookers).

Sit and ***down***—the two control commands—prevent or resolve nearly a hundred behavior problems. For example, if the dog happily and obediently sits or lies down when requested, she cannot jump on visitors, dash out the front door, run around and chase her tail, pester other dogs, harass cats or annoy family, friends or strangers. Additionally, "Sit" or "Down" are the best emergency commands for off-leash control.

It is easier to teach and maintain a reliable sit than maintain a reliable recall. *Sit* is the purest and simplest of commands—either the dog is sitting or she is not. If there is any change of circumstances or potential danger in the park, for example, simply instruct the dog to sit. If she sits, you have a number of options: Allow the dog to resume playing when she is safe, walk up and put the dog on leash or call the dog. The dog will be much more likely to come when called if she has already acknowledged her compliance by sitting. If the dog does not sit in the park—train her to!

Stand and ***rollover-stay*** are the two positions for examining the dog. Your veterinarian will love you to distraction if you take a little time to teach the dog to stand still and roll over and play possum. Also, your vet bills will be smaller because it will take the veterinarian less time to examine your dog. The rollover-stay is an especially useful command and is really just a variation of the down-stay: Whereas the dog lies prone in the traditional down, she lies supine in the rollover-stay.

As with teaching come and sit, the training techniques to teach the dog to assume all other body positions on cue are user-friendly and dog-friendly. Simply give the appropriate request, lure the dog into the desired body position using a training treat or toy and then *praise* (and maybe reward) the dog as soon as she complies. Try not to touch the dog to get her to respond. If you teach the dog by guiding her into position, the dog will quickly learn that rump-pressure means sit, for example, but as yet you still have no control over your dog if she is just 6 feet away. It will still be necessary to teach the dog to sit on request. So do not make training a time-consuming two-step process; instead, teach the dog to sit to a verbal request or hand signal from the outset. Once the dog sits willingly when requested, by all means use your hands to pet the dog when she does so.

To teach **down** when the dog is already sitting, say "Tina, down!," hold the lure in one hand (palm down) and lower that hand to the floor between the dog's forepaws. As the dog lowers her head to follow the lure, slowly move the lure away from the dog just a fraction (in front of her paws). The dog will lie down as she stretches her nose forward to follow the lure. Praise the dog when she does so. If the dog stands up, you pulled the lure away too far and too quickly.

When teaching the dog to lie down from the standing position, say "Down" and lower the lure to the floor as before. Once the dog has lowered her forequarters and assumed a play bow, gently and slowly move the lure *towards* the dog between her forelegs. Praise the dog as soon as her rear end plops down.

After just a couple of trials it will be possible to alternate sits and downs and have the dog energetically perform doggy push-ups. Praise the dog a lot, and after half a dozen or so push-ups reward the dog with a training treat or toy. You will notice the more energetically you move your arm—upwards (palm up) to get the dog to sit, and downwards (palm down) to get the dog to lie down—the more energetically the dog responds to your requests. Now try training the dog in silence and you will notice she has also learned to respond to hand signals. Yeah! Not too shabby for the first session.

To teach **stand** from the sitting position, say "Tina, stand," slowly move the lure half a dog-length away from the dog's nose, keeping it at nose level, and praise the dog as she stands to follow the lure. As soon

Using a food lure to teach sit, down and stand. 1) "Phoenix, sit." 2) Hand palm upwards, move lure up and back over dog's muzzle. 3) "Good sit, Phoenix!" 4) "Phoenix, down." 5) Hand palm downwards, move lure down to lie between dog's forepaws. 6) "Phoenix, off. Good down, Phoenix!" 7) "Phoenix, sit!" 8) Palm upwards, move lure up and back, keeping it close to dog's muzzle. 9) "Good sit, Phoenix!"

10) *"Phoenix, stand!"* 11) *Move lure away from dog at nose height, then lower it a tad.* 12) *"Phoenix, off! Good stand, Phoenix!"* 13) *"Phoenix, down!"* 14) *Hand palm downwards, move lure down to lie between dog's forepaws.* 15) *"Phoenix, off! Good down-stay, Phoenix!"* 16) *"Phoenix, stand!"* 17) *Move lure away from dog's muzzle up to nose height.* 18) *"Phoenix, off! Good stand-stay, Phoenix. Now we'll make the vet and groomer happy!"*

as the dog stands, lower the lure to just beneath the dog's chin to entice her to look down; otherwise she will stand and then sit immediately. To prompt the dog to stand from the down position, move the lure half a dog-length upwards and away from the dog, holding the lure at standing nose height from the floor.

Teaching *rollover* is best started from the down position, with the dog lying on one side, or at least with both hind legs stretched out on the same side. Say "Tina, bang!" and move the lure backwards and alongside the dog's muzzle to her elbow (on the side of her outstretched hind legs). Once the dog looks to the side and backwards, very slowly move the lure upwards to the dog's shoulder and backbone. Tickling the dog in the goolies (groin area) often invokes a reflex-raising of the hind leg as an appeasement gesture, which facilitates the tendency to roll over. If you move the lure too quickly and the dog jumps into the standing position, have patience and start again. As soon as the dog rolls onto her back, keep the lure stationary and mesmerize the dog with a relaxing tummy rub.

To teach *rollover-stay* when the dog is standing or moving, say "Tina, bang!" and give the appropriate hand signal (with index finger pointed and thumb cocked in true Sam Spade fashion), then in one fluid movement lure her to first lie down and then rollover-stay as above.

Teaching the dog to *stay* in each of the above four positions becomes a piece of cake after first teaching the dog not to worry at the toy or treat training lure. This is best accomplished by hand feeding dinner kibble. Hold a piece of kibble firmly in your hand and softly instruct "Off!" Ignore any licking and slobbering *for however long the dog worries at the treat*, but say "Take it!" and offer the kibble *the instant* the dog breaks contact with her muzzle. Repeat this a few times, and then up the ante and insist the dog remove her muzzle for one whole second before offering the kibble. Then progressively refine your criteria and have the dog not touch your hand (or treat) for longer and longer periods on each trial, such as for two seconds, four seconds, then six, ten, fifteen, twenty, thirty seconds and so on.

The dog soon learns: (1) worrying at the treat never gets results, whereas (2) noncontact is often rewarded after a variable time lapse.

Teaching *"Off!"* has many useful applications in its own right. Additionally, instructing the dog not to touch a training lure often produces spontaneous and magical stays. Request the dog to stand-stay, for example, and not to touch the lure. At first set your sights on a short two-second stay before rewarding the dog. (Remember, every long journey begins with a single step.) However, on subsequent trials, gradually and progressively increase the length of stay required to receive a reward. In no time at all your dog will stand calmly for a minute or so.

Relevancy Training

Once you have taught the dog what you expect her to do when requested to come, sit, lie down, stand, rollover and stay, the time is right to teach the dog *why* she should comply with your wishes. The secret is to have many (*many*) extremely short training interludes (two to five seconds each) at numerous (*numerous*) times during the course of the dog's day. Especially work with the dog immediately *before* the dog's good times and *during* the dog's good times. For example, ask your dog to sit and/or lie down each time before opening doors, serving meals, offering treats and tummy rubs; ask the dog to perform a few controlled doggy push-ups before letting her off leash or throwing a tennis ball; and perhaps request the dog to sit-down-sit-stand-down-stand-rollover before inviting her to cuddle on the couch.

Similarly, request the dog to sit many times during play or on walks, and in no time at all the dog will be only too pleased to follow your instructions because she has learned that a compliant response heralds all sorts of goodies. Basically all you are trying to teach the dog is how to say please: "Please throw the tennis ball. Please may I snuggle on the couch."

Remember, it is important to keep training interludes short and to have many short sessions each and every day. The shortest (and most useful) session comprises asking the dog to sit and then go play during a play session. When trained this way, your dog will soon associate training with good times. In fact, the dog may be unable to distinguish between training and good times and, indeed, there should be no distinction. The warped concept that training involves forcing the dog to comply and/or dominating her will is totally at odds with the picture of a truly well-trained dog. In reality, enjoying a game of training with a dog is no different from enjoying a game of backgammon or tennis with a friend; and walking with a dog should be no different from strolling with a spouse, or with buddies on the golf course.

Walk by Your Side

Many people attempt to teach a dog to heel by putting her on a leash and physically correcting the dog when she makes mistakes. There are a number of things seriously wrong with this approach, the first being that most people do not want precision heeling; rather, they simply want the dog to follow or walk by their side. Second, when physically restrained during "training," even though the dog may grudgingly mope by your side when "handcuffed" on leash, let's see what happens when she is off leash. History! The dog is in the next county because she never enjoyed walking with you on leash and you have no control over her off leash. So let's just teach the dog off leash from the outset to *want* to walk with us. Third, if the dog has not been trained to heel, it is a trifle hasty to think about punishing the poor dog for making mistakes and breaking heeling rules she didn't even know existed. This is simply not fair! Surely, if the dog had been adequately taught how to heel, she would seldom make mistakes and hence there would be no need to correct the dog. Remember, each mistake and each correction (punishment) advertise the trainer's inadequacy, not the dog's. The dog is not stubborn, she is not stupid and she is not bad. Even if she were, she would still require training, so let's train her properly.

Let's teach the dog to *enjoy* following us and to *want* to walk by our side off leash. Then it will be easier to teach high-precision off-leash heeling patterns if desired. Before going on outdoor walks, it is necessary to teach the dog not to pull. Then it becomes easy to teach on-leash walking and heeling because the dog already wants to walk with you, she is familiar with the desired walking and heeling positions and she knows not to pull.

FOLLOWING

Start by training your dog to follow you. Many puppies will follow if you simply walk away from them and maybe click your fingers or chuckle. Adult dogs may require additional enticement to stimulate them to follow, such as a training lure or, at the very least, a lively trainer. To teach the dog to follow: (1) keep walking and (2) walk away from the dog. If the dog attempts to lead or lag, change pace; slow down if the dog forges too far ahead, but speed up if she lags too far behind. Say "Steady!" or "Easy!" each time before you slow down and "Quickly!" or "Hustle!" each time before you speed up, and the dog will learn to change pace on cue. If the dog lags or leads too far, or if she wanders right or left, simply walk quickly in the opposite direction and maybe even run away from the dog and hide.

Practicing is a lot of fun; you can set up a course in your home, yard or park to do this. Indoors, entice the dog to follow upstairs, into a bedroom, into the bathroom, downstairs, around the living room couch, zigzagging between dining room chairs and into the kitchen for dinner. Outdoors, get the dog to follow around park benches, trees, shrubs and along walkways and lines in the grass. (For safety outdoors, it is advisable to attach a long line on the dog, but never exert corrective tension on the line.)

121

Remember, following has a lot to do with attitude—
your attitude! Most probably your dog will *not* want to
follow Mr. Grumpy Troll with the personality of wilted
lettuce. Lighten up—walk with a jaunty step, whistle a
happy tune, sing, skip and tell jokes to your dog and
she will be right there by your side.

BY YOUR SIDE

It is smart to train the dog to walk close on one side or
the other—either side will do, your choice. When walking, jogging or cycling, it is generally bad news to have
the dog suddenly cut in front of you. In fact, I train my
dogs to walk "By my side" and "Other side"—both very
useful instructions. It is possible to position the dog
fairly accurately by looking to the appropriate side and
clicking your fingers or slapping your thigh on that
side. A precise positioning may be attained by holding
a training lure, such as a chew toy, tennis ball or food
treat. Stop and stand still several times throughout the
walk, just as you would when window shopping or
meeting a friend. Use the lure to make sure the dog
slows down and stays close whenever you stop.

When teaching the dog to heel, we generally want
her to sit in heel position when we stop. Teach heel

*Using a toy to teach sit-heel-sit sequences: 1) "Phoenix, sit!" Standing still, move lure up and back over dog's
muzzle . . . 2) to position dog sitting in heel position on your left side. 3) Say "Phoenix, heel!" and walk ahead,
wagging lure in left hand. Change lure to right hand in preparation for sit signal. Say "Sit" and then . . .*

122

position at the standstill and the dog will learn that the default heel position is sitting by your side (left or right—your choice, unless you wish to compete in obedience trials, in which case the dog must heel on the left).

Several times a day, stand up and call your dog to come and sit in heel position—"Tina, heel!" For example, instruct the dog to come to heel each time there are commercials on TV, or each time you turn a page of a novel, and the dog will get it in a single evening.

Practice straight-line heeling and turns separately. With the dog sitting at heel, teach her to turn in place. After each quarter-turn, half-turn or full turn in place, lure the dog to sit at heel. Now it's time for short straight-line heeling sequences, no more than a few steps at a time. Always think of heeling in terms of sit-heel-sit sequences—start and end with the dog in position and do your best to keep her there when moving. Progressively increase the number of steps in each sequence. When the dog remains close for 20 yards of straight-line heeling, it is time to add a few turns and then sign up for a happy-heeling obedience class to get some advice from the experts.

4) use hand signal to lure dog to sit as you stop. Eventually, dog will sit automatically at heel whenever you stop. 5) "Good dog!"

No Pulling on Leash

You can start teaching your dog not to pull on leash anywhere—in front of the television or outdoors—but regardless of location, you must not take a single step with tension in the leash. For a reason known only to dogs, even just a couple of paces of pulling on leash is intrinsically motivating and diabolically rewarding. Instead, attach the leash to the dog's collar, grasp the other end firmly with both hands held close to your chest, and stand still—do not budge an inch. Have somebody watch you with a stopwatch to time your progress, or else you will never believe this will work and so you will not even try the exercise, and your shoulder and the dog's neck will be traumatized for years to come.

Stand still and wait for the dog to stop pulling, and to sit and/or lie down. All dogs stop pulling and sit eventually. Most take only a couple of minutes; the all-time record is $22\frac{1}{2}$ minutes. Time how long it takes. Gently praise the dog when she stops pulling, and as soon as she sits, enthusiastically praise the dog and take just one step forward, then immediately stand still. This single step usually demonstrates the ballistic reinforcing nature of pulling on leash; most dogs explode to the end of the leash, so be prepared for the strain. Stand firm and wait for the dog to sit again. Repeat this half a dozen times and you will probably notice a progressive reduction in the force of the dog's one-step explosions and a radical reduction in the time it takes for the dog to sit each time.

As the dog learns "Sit we go" and "Pull we stop," she will begin to walk forward calmly with each single step and automatically sit when you stop. Now try two steps before you stop. Wooooooo! Scary! When the dog has mastered two steps at a time, try for three. After each success, progressively increase the number of steps in the sequence: try four steps and then six, eight, ten and twenty steps before stopping. Congratulations! You are now walking the dog on leash.

Whenever walking with the dog (off leash or on leash), make sure you stop periodically to practice a few position commands and stays before instructing the dog to "Walk on!" (Remember, you want the dog to be compliant everywhere, not just in the kitchen when her dinner is at hand.) For example, stopping every 25 yards to briefly train the dog amounts to over 200 training interludes within a single 3-mile stroll. And each training session is in a different location. You will not believe the improvement within just the first mile of the first walk.

To put it another way, integrating training into a walk offers 200 separate opportunities to use the continuance of the walk as a reward to reinforce the dog's education. Moreover, some training interludes may comprise continuing education for the dog's walking skills: Alternate short periods of the dog walking calmly by your side with periods when the dog is allowed to sniff and investigate the environment. Now sniffing odors on the grass and meeting other dogs become rewards which reinforce the dog's calm and mannerly demeanor. Good Lord! Whatever next? Many enjoyable walks together of course. Happy trails!

THE IMPORTANCE OF TRICKS

Nothing will improve a dog's quality of life better than having a few tricks under her belt. Teaching any trick expands the dog's vocabulary, which facilitates communication and improves the owner's control. Also, specific tricks help prevent and resolve specific behavior problems. For example, by teaching the dog to fetch her toys, the dog learns carrying a toy makes the owner happy and, therefore, will be more likely to chew her toy than other inappropriate items.

More important, teaching tricks prompts owners to lighten up and train with a sunny disposition. Really, tricks should be no different from any other behaviors we put on cue. But they are. When teaching tricks, owners have a much sweeter attitude, which in turn motivates the dog and improves her willingness to comply. The dog feels tricks are a blast, but formal commands are a drag. In fact, tricks are so enjoyable, they may be used as rewards in training by asking the dog to come, sit and down-stay and then rollover for a tummy rub. Go on, try it: Crack a smile and even giggle when the dog promptly and willingly lies down and stays.

Most important, performing tricks prompts onlookers to smile and giggle. Many people are scared of dogs, especially large ones. And nothing can be more off-putting for a dog than to be constantly confronted by strangers who don't like her because of her size or the way she looks. Uneasy people put the dog on edge, causing her to back off and bark, only frightening people all the more. And so a vicious circle develops, with the people's fear fueling the dog's fear *and vice versa*. Instead, tie a pink ribbon to your dog's collar and practice all sorts of tricks on walks and in the park, and you will be pleasantly amazed how it changes people's attitudes toward your friendly dog. The dog's repertoire of tricks is limited only by the trainer's imagination. Below I have described three of my favorites:

SPEAK AND SHUSH

The training sequence involved in teaching a dog to bark on request is no different from that used when training any behavior on cue: request—lure—response—reward. As always, the secret of success lies in finding an effective lure. If the dog always barks at the doorbell, for example, say "Rover, speak!", have an accomplice ring the doorbell, then reward the dog for barking. After a few woofs, ask Rover to "Shush!", waggle a food treat under her nose (to entice her to sniff and thus to shush), praise her when quiet and eventually offer the treat as a reward. Alternate "Speak" and "Shush," progressively increasing the length of shush-time between each barking bout.

PLAY BOW

With the dog standing, say "Bow!" and lower the food lure (palm upwards) to rest between the dog's forepaws. Praise as the dog lowers her forequarters and sternum to the ground (as when teaching the down), but then lure the dog to stand and offer the treat. On successive trials, gradually increase the length of time the dog is required to remain in the play bow posture in order to gain a food reward. If the dog's rear end collapses into a down, say nothing and offer no reward; simply start over.

BE A BEAR

With the dog sitting backed into a corner to prevent her from toppling over backwards, say "Be a bear!" With bent paw and palm down, raise a lure upwards and backwards along the top of the dog's muzzle. Praise the dog when she sits up on her haunches and offer the treat as a reward. To prevent the dog from standing on her hind legs, keep the lure closer to the dog's muzzle. On each trial, progressively increase the length of time the dog is required to sit up to receive a food reward. Since lure-reward training is so easy, teach the dog to stand and walk on her hind legs as well!

Teaching "Be a Bear"

127

chapter 9

Getting
Active
with your Dog

by Bardi McLennan

Once you and your dog have graduated from basic obedience training and are beginning to work together as a team, you can take part in the growing world of dog activities. There are so many fun things to do with your dog! Just remember, people and dogs don't always learn at the same pace, so don't be upset if you (or your dog) need more than two basic training courses before your team becomes operational. Even smart dogs don't go straight to college from kindergarten!

Just as there are events geared to certain types of dogs, so there are ones that are more appealing to certain types of people. In some

128

activities, you give the commands and your dog does the work (upland game hunting is one example), while in others, such as agility, you'll both get a workout. You may want to aim for prestigious titles to add to your dog's name, or you may want nothing more than the sheer enjoyment of being around other people and their dogs. Passive or active, participation has its own rewards.

Consider your dog's physical capabilities when looking into any of the canine activities. It's easy to see that a Basset Hound is not built for the racetrack, nor would a Chihuahua be the breed of choice for pulling a sled. A loyal dog will attempt almost anything you ask him to do, so it is up to you to know your dog's limitations. A dog must be physically sound in order to compete at any level in athletic activities, and being mentally sound is a definite plus. Advanced age, however, may not be a deterrent. Many dogs still hunt and herd at ten or twelve years of age. It's entirely possible for dogs to be "fit at 50." Take your dog for a checkup, explain to your vet the type of activity you have in mind and be guided by his or her findings.

All dogs seem to love playing flyball.

You needn't be restricted to breed-specific sports if it's only fun you're after. Certain AKC activities are limited to designated breeds; however, as each new trial, test or sport has grown in popularity, so has the variety of breeds encouraged to participate at a fun level.

But don't shortchange your fun, or that of your dog, by thinking only of the basic function of her breed. Once a dog has learned how to learn, she can be taught to do just about anything as long as the size of the dog is right for the job and you both think it is fun and rewarding. In other words, you are a team.

To get involved in any of the activities detailed in this chapter, look for the names and addresses of the organizations that sponsor them in Chapter 13. You can also ask your breeder or a local dog trainer for contacts.

You can compete in obedience trials with a well trained dog.

Official American Kennel Club Activities

The following tests and trials are some of the events sanctioned by the AKC and sponsored by various dog clubs. Your dog's expertise will be rewarded with impressive titles. You can participate just for fun, or be competitive and go for those awards.

OBEDIENCE

Training classes begin with pups as young as three months of age in kindergarten puppy training, then advance to pre-novice (all exercises on lead) and go on to novice, which is where you'll start off-lead work. In obedience classes dogs learn to sit, stay, heel and come through a variety of exercises. Once you've got the basics down, you can enter obedience trials and work toward earning your dog's first degree, a C.D. (Companion Dog).

The next level is called "Open," in which jumps and retrieves perk up the dog's interest. Passing grades in competition at this level earn a C.D.X. (Companion Dog Excellent). Beyond that lies the goal of the most ambitious—Utility (U.D. and even U.D.X. or OTCh, an Obedience Champion).

AGILITY

All dogs can participate in the latest canine sport to have gained worldwide popularity for its fun and excitement, agility. It began in England as a canine version of horse show-jumping, but because dogs are more agile and able to perform on verbal commands, extra feats were added such as climbing, balancing and racing through tunnels or in and out of weave poles. Many of the obstacles (regulation or homemade) can be set up in your own backyard. If the agility bug bites, you could end up in international competition!

For starters, your dog should be obedience trained, even though, in the beginning, the lessons may all be taught on lead. Once the dog understands the commands (and you do, too), it's as easy as guiding the dog over a prescribed course, one obstacle at a time. In competition, the race is against the clock, so wear your running shoes! The dog starts with 200 points and the judge deducts for infractions and misadventures along the way.

All dogs seem to love agility and respond to it as if they were being turned loose in a playground paradise. Your dog's enthusiasm will be contagious; agility turns into great fun for dog and owner.

FIELD TRIALS AND HUNTING TESTS

There are field trials and hunting tests for the sporting breeds—retrievers, spaniels and pointing breeds, and for some hounds—Bassets, Beagles and Dachshunds. Field trials are competitive events that test a dog's ability to perform the functions for which she was bred. Hunting tests, which are open to retrievers,

---

TITLES AWARDED BY THE AKC

Conformation: Ch. (Champion)

Obedience: CD (Companion Dog); CDX (Companion Dog Excellent); UD (Utility Dog); UDX (Utility Dog Excellent); OTCh. (Obedience Trial Champion)

Field: JH (Junior Hunter); SH (Senior Hunter); MH (Master Hunter); AFCh. (Amateur Field Champion); FCh. (Field Champion)

Lure Coursing: JC (Junior Courser); SC (Senior Courser)

Herding: HT (Herding Tested); PT (Pre-Trial Tested); HS (Herding Started); HI (Herding Intermediate); HX (Herding Excellent); HCh. (Herding Champion)

Tracking: TD (Tracking Dog); TDX (Tracking Dog Excellent)

Agility: NAD (Novice Agility); OAD (Open Agility); ADX (Agility Excellent); MAX (Master Agility)

Earthdog Tests: JE (Junior Earthdog); SE (Senior Earthdog); ME (Master Earthdog)

Canine Good Citizen: CGC

Combination: DC (Dual Champion—Ch. and Fch.); TC (Triple Champion—Ch., Fch., and OTCh.)

---

spaniels and pointing breeds only, are noncompetitive and are a means of judging the dog's ability as well as that of the handler.

Hunting is a very large and complex part of canine sports, and if you own one of the breeds that hunts, the events are a great treat for your dog and you. He gets to do what he was bred for, and you get to work with him and watch him do it. You'll be proud of and amazed at what your dog can do.

Fortunately, the AKC publishes a series of booklets on these events, which outline the rules and regulations and include a glossary of the sometimes complicated terms. The AKC also publishes newsletters for field trialers and hunting test enthusiasts. The United Kennel Club (UKC) also has informative materials for the hunter and his dog.

Retrievers and other sporting breeds get to do what they're bred to in hunting tests.

HERDING TESTS AND TRIALS

Herding, like hunting, dates back to the first known uses man made of dogs. The interest in herding today is widespread, and if you own a herding breed, you can join in the activity. Herding dogs are tested for their natural skills to keep a flock of ducks, sheep or cattle together. If your dog shows potential, you can start at the testing level, where your dog can earn a title for showing an inherent herding ability. With training you can advance to the trial level, where your dog should be capable of controlling even difficult livestock in diverse situations.

LURE COURSING

The AKC Tests and Trials for Lure Coursing are open to traditional sighthounds—Greyhounds, Whippets,

Borzoi, Salukis, Afghan Hounds, Ibizan Hounds and Scottish Deerhounds—as well as to Basenjis and Rhodesian Ridgebacks. Hounds are judged on overall ability, follow, speed, agility and endurance. This is possibly the most exciting of the trials for spectators, because the speed and agility of the dogs is awesome to watch as they chase the lure (or "course") in heats of two or three dogs at a time.

TRACKING

This tracking dog is hot on the trail.

Tracking is another activity in which almost any dog can compete because every dog that sniffs the ground when taken outdoors is, in fact, tracking. The hard part comes when the rules as to what, when and where the dog tracks are determined by a person, not the dog! Tracking tests cover a large area of fields, woods and roads. The tracks are laid hours before the dogs go to work on them, and include "tricks" like cross-tracks and sharp turns. If you're interested in search-and-rescue work, this is the place to start.

EARTHDOG TESTS FOR SMALL TERRIERS AND DACHSHUNDS

These tests are open to Australian, Bedlington, Border, Cairn, Dandie Dinmont, Smooth and Wire Fox, Lakeland, Norfolk, Norwich, Scottish, Sealyham, Skye, Welsh and West Highland White Terriers as well as Dachshunds. The dogs need no prior training for this terrier sport. There is a qualifying test on the day of the event, so dog and handler learn the rules on the spot. These tests, or "digs," sometimes end with informal races in the late afternoon.

Here are some of the extracurricular obedience and racing activities that are not regulated by the AKC or UKC, but are generally run by clubs or a group of dog fanciers and are often open to all.

Canine Freestyle This activity is something new on the scene and is variously likened to dancing, dressage or ice skating. It is meant to show the athleticism of the dog, but also requires showmanship on the part of the dog's handler. If you and your dog like to ham it up for friends, you might want to look into freestyle.

Lure coursing lets sighthounds do what they do best—run!

Scent Hurdle Racing Scent hurdle racing is purely a fun activity sponsored by obedience clubs with members forming competing teams. The height of the hurdles is based on the size of the shortest dog on the team. On a signal, one team dog is released on each of two side-by-side courses and must clear every hurdle before picking up its own dumbbell from a platform and returning over the jumps to the handler. As each dog returns, the next on that team is sent. Of course, that is what the dogs are supposed to do. When the dogs improvise (going under or around the hurdles, stealing another dog's dumbbell, and so forth), it no doubt frustrates the handlers, but just adds to the fun for everyone else.

Flyball This type of racing is similar, but after negotiating the four hurdles, the dog comes to a flyball box, steps on a lever that releases a tennis ball into the air, catches the ball and returns over the hurdles to the starting point. This game also becomes extremely fun for spectators because the dogs sometimes cheat by catching a ball released by the dog in the next lane. Three titles can be earned—Flyball Dog (F.D.), Flyball Dog Excellent (F.D.X.) and Flyball Dog Champion (Fb.D.Ch.)—all awarded by the North American Flyball Association, Inc.

Dogsledding The name conjures up the Rocky Mountains or the frigid North, but you can find dogsled clubs in such unlikely spots as Maryland, North Carolina and Virginia! Dogsledding is primarily for the Nordic breeds such as the Alaskan Malamutes, Siberian Huskies and Samoyeds, but other breeds can try. There are some practical backyard applications to this sport, too. With parental supervision, almost any strong dog could pull a child's sled.

Coming over the A-frame on an agility course.

These are just some of the many recreational ways you can get to know and understand your multifaceted dog better and have fun doing it.

10

Your Dog
and your
Family

by Bardi McLennan

Adding a dog automatically increases your family by one, no matter whether you live alone in an apartment or are part of a mother, father and six kids household. The single-person family is fair game for numerous and varied canine misconceptions as to who is dog and who pays the bills, whereas a dog in a houseful of children will consider himself to be just one of the gang, littermates all. One dog and one child may give a dog reason to believe they are both kids or both dogs.

Either interpretation requires parental supervision and sometimes speedy intervention.

As soon as one paw goes through the door into your home, Rufus (or Rufina) has to make many adjustments to become a part of your family. Your job is to make him fit in as painlessly as possible. An older dog may have some frame of reference from past experience, but to a 10-week-old puppy, everything is brand new: people, furniture, stairs, when and where people eat, sleep or watch TV, his own place and everyone else's space, smells, sounds, outdoors—everything!

Puppies, and newly acquired dogs of any age, do not need what we think of as "freedom." If you leave a new dog or puppy loose in the house, you will almost certainly return to chaotic destruction and the dog will forever after equate your homecoming with a time of punishment to be dreaded. It is unfair to give your dog what amounts to "freedom to get into trouble." Instead, confine him to a crate for brief periods of your absence (up to three or four hours) and, for the long haul, a workday for example, confine him to one untrashable area with his own toys, a bowl of water and a radio left on (low) in another room.

Lots of pets get along with each other just fine.

For the first few days, when not confined, put Rufus on a long leash tied to your wrist or waist. This umbilical cord method enables the dog to learn all about you from your body language and voice, and to learn by his own actions which things in the house are NO! and which ones are rewarded by "Good dog." Housetraining will be easier with the pup always by your side. Speaking of which, accidents do happen. That goal of "completely housetrained" takes up to a year, or the length of time it takes the pup to mature.

The All-Adult Family

Most dogs in an adults-only household today are likely to be latchkey pets, with no one home all day but the dog. When you return after a tough day on the job, the dog can and should be your relaxation therapy. But going home can instead be a daily frustration.

Separation anxiety is a very common problem for the dog in a working household. It may begin with whines and barks of loneliness, but it will soon escalate into a frenzied destruction derby. That is why it is so important to set aside the time to teach a dog to relax when left alone in his confined area and to understand that he can trust you to return.

Let the dog get used to your work schedule in easy stages. Confine him to one room and go in and out of that room over and over again. Be casual about it. No physical, voice or eye contact. When the pup no longer even notices your comings and goings, leave the house for varying lengths of time, returning to stay home for a few minutes and gradually increasing the time away. This training can take days, but the dog is learning that you haven't left him forever and that he can trust you.

Any time you leave the dog, but especially during this training period, be casual about your departure. No anxiety-building fond farewells. Just "Bye" and go! Remember the "Good dog" when you return to find everything more or less as you left it.

If things are a mess (or even a disaster) when you return, greet the dog, take him outside to eliminate, and then put him in his crate while you clean up. Rant and rave in the shower! *Do not* punish the dog. You were not there when it happened, and the rule is: Only punish as you catch the dog in the act of wrongdoing. Obviously, it makes sense to get your latchkey puppy when you'll have a week or two to spend on these training essentials.

Family weekend activities should include Rufus whenever possible. Depending on the pup's age, now is the time for a long walk in the park, playtime in the backyard, a hike in the woods. Socializing is as important as health care, good food and physical exercise, so visiting Aunt Emma or Uncle Harry and the next-door neighbor's dog or cat is essential to developing an outgoing, friendly temperament in your pet.

If you are a single adult, socializing Rufus at home and away will prevent him from becoming overly protective of you (or just overly attached) and will also prevent such behavioral problems as dominance or fear of strangers.

Babies

Whether already here or on the way, babies figure larger than life in the eyes of a dog. If the dog is there first, let him in on all your baby preparations in the house. When baby arrives, let Rufus sniff any item of clothing that has been on the baby before Junior comes home. Then let Mom greet the dog first before introducing the new family member. Hold the baby down for the dog to see and sniff, but make sure someone's holding the dog on lead in case of any sudden moves. Don't play keep-away or tease the dog with the baby, which only invites undesirable jumping up.

The dog and the baby are "family," and for starters can be treated almost as equals. Things rapidly change, however, especially when baby takes to creeping around on all fours on the dog's turf or, better yet, has yummy pudding all over her face and hands! That's when a lot of things in the dog's and baby's lives become more separate than equal.

Dogs are perfect confidants.

Toddlers make terrible dog owners, but if you can't avoid the combination, use patient discipline (that is, positive teaching rather than punishment), and use time-outs before you run out of patience.

139

A dog and a baby (or toddler, or an assertive young child) should never be left alone together. Take the dog with you or confine him. With a baby or youngsters in the house, you'll have plenty of use for that wonderful canine safety device called a crate!

Young Children

Any dog in a house with kids will behave pretty much as the kids do, good or bad. But even good dogs and good children can get into trouble when play becomes rowdy and active.

Teach children how to play nicely with a puppy.

Legs bobbing up and down, shrill voices screeching, a ball hurtling overhead, all add up to exuberant frustration for a dog who's just trying to be part of the gang. In a pack of puppies, any legs or toys being chased would be caught by a set of teeth, and all the pups involved would understand that is how the game is played. Kids do not understand this, nor do parents tolerate it. Bring Rufus indoors before you have reason to regret it. This is time-out, not a punishment.

You can explain the situation to the children and tell them they must play quieter games until the puppy learns not to grab them with his mouth. Unfortunately, you can't explain it that easily to the dog. With adult supervision, they will learn how to play together.

Young children love to tease. Sticking their faces or wiggling their hands or fingers in the dog's face is teasing. To another person it might be just annoying, but it is threatening to a dog. There's another difference: We can make the child stop by an explanation, but the only way a dog can stop it is with a warning growl and then with teeth. Teasing is the major cause of children being bitten by their pets. Treat it seriously.

140

Older Children

The best age for a child to get a first dog is between the ages of 8 and 12. That's when kids are able to accept some real responsibility for their pet. Even so, take the child's vow of "I will never *ever* forget to feed (brush, walk, etc.) the dog" for what it's worth: a child's good intention at that moment. Most kids today have extra lessons, soccer practice, Little League, ballet, and so forth piled on top of school schedules. There will be many times when Mom will have to come to the dog's rescue. "I walked the dog for you so you can set the table for me" is one way to get around a missed appointment without laying on blame or guilt.

Kids in this age group make excellent obedience trainers because they are into the teaching/learning process themselves and they lack the self-consciousness of adults. Attending a dog show is something the whole family can enjoy, and watching Junior Showmanship may catch the eye of the kids. Older children can begin to get involved in many of the recreational activities that were reviewed in the previous chapter. Some of the agility obstacles, for example, can be set up in the backyard as a family project (with an adult making sure all the equipment is safe and secure for the dog).

Older kids are also beginning to look to the future, and may envision themselves as veterinarians or trainers or show dog handlers or writers of the next Lassie best-seller. Dogs are perfect confidants for these dreams. They won't tell a soul.

Other Pets

Introduce all pets tactfully. In a dog/cat situation, hold the dog, not the cat. Let two dogs meet on neutral turf—a stroll in the park or a walk down the street—with both on loose leads to permit all the normal canine ways of saying hello, including routine sniffing, circling, more sniffing, and so on. Small creatures such as hamsters, chinchillas or mice must be kept safe from their natural predators (dogs and cats).

Festive Family Occasions

Parties are great for people, but not necessarily for puppies. Until all the guests have arrived, put the dog in his crate or in a room where he won't be disturbed. A socialized dog can join the fun later as long as he's not underfoot, annoying guests or into the hors d'oeuvres.

There are a few dangers to consider, too. Doors opening and closing can allow a puppy to slip out unnoticed in the confusion, and you'll be organizing a search party instead of playing host or hostess. Party food and buffet service are not for dogs. Let Rufus party in his crate with a nice big dog biscuit.

At Christmas time, not only are tree decorations dangerous and breakable (and perhaps family heirlooms), but extreme caution should be taken with the lights, cords and outlets for the tree lights and any other festive lighting. Occasionally a dog lifts a leg, ignoring the fact that the tree is indoors. To avoid this, use a canine repellent, made for gardens, on the tree. Or keep him out of the tree room unless supervised. And whatever you do, *don't* invite trouble by hanging his toys on the tree!

Car Travel

Before you plan a vacation by car or RV with Rufus, be sure he enjoys car travel. Nothing spoils a holiday quicker than a carsick dog! Work within the dog's comfort level. Get in the car with the dog in his crate or attached to a canine car safety belt and just sit there until he relaxes. That's all. Next time, get in the car, turn on the engine and go nowhere. Just sit. When that is okay, turn on the engine and go around the block. Now you can go for a ride and include a stop where you get out, leaving the dog for a minute or two.

On a warm day, always park in the shade and leave windows open several inches. And return quickly. It only takes 10 minutes for a car to become an overheated steel death trap.

Motel or Pet Motel?

Not all motels or hotels accept pets, but you have a much better choice today than even a few years ago. To find a dog-friendly lodging, look at *On the Road Again With Man's Best Friend*, a series of directories that detail bed and breakfasts, inns, family resorts and other hotels/motels. Some places require a refundable deposit to cover any damage incurred by the dog. More B&Bs accept pets now, but some restrict the size.

If taking Rufus with you is not feasible, check out boarding kennels in your area. Your veterinarian may offer this service, or recommend a kennel or two he or she is familiar with. Go see the facilities for yourself, ask about exercise, diet, housing, and so on. Or, if you'd rather have Rufus stay home, look into bonded petsitters, many of whom will also bring in the mail and water your plants.

chapter 11

Your Dog
and your
Community

by Bardi McLennan

Step outside your home with your dog and you are no longer just family, you are both part of your community. This is when the phrase "responsible pet ownership" takes on serious implications. For starters, it means you pick up after your dog—not just occasionally, but every time your dog eliminates away from home. That means you have joined the Plastic Baggy Brigade! You always have plastic sandwich bags in your pocket and several in the car. It means you teach your kids how to use them, too. If you think this is "yucky," just imagine what

the person (a non-doggy person) who inadvertently steps in the mess thinks!

Your responsibility extends to your neighbors: To their ears (no annoying barking); to their property (their garbage, their lawn, their flower beds, their cat—especially their cat); to their kids (on bikes, at play); to their kids' toys and sports equipment.

There are numerous dog-related laws, ranging from simple dog licensing and leash laws to those holding you liable for any physical injury or property damage done by your dog. These laws are in place to protect everyone in the community, including you and your dog. There are town ordinances and state laws which are by no means the same in all towns or all states. Ignorance of the law won't get you off the hook. The time to find out what the laws are where you live is now.

Be sure your dog's license is current. This is not just a good local ordinance, it can make the difference between finding your lost dog or not.

Dressing your dog up makes him appealing to strangers.

Many states now require proof of rabies vaccination and that the dog has been spayed or neutered before issuing a license. At the same time, keep up the dog's annual immunizations.

Never let your dog run loose in the neighborhood. This will not only keep you on the right side of the leash law, it's the outdoor version of the rule about not giving your dog "freedom to get into trouble."

Good Canine Citizen

Sometimes it's hard for a dog's owner to assess whether or not the dog is sufficiently socialized to be accepted by the community at large. Does Rufus or Rufina display good, controlled behavior in public? The AKC's Canine Good Citizen program is available through many dog organizations. If your dog passes the test, the title "CGC" is earned.

The overall purpose is to turn your dog into a good neighbor and to teach you about your responsibility to your community as a dog owner. Here are the ten things your dog must do willingly:

1. Accept a stranger stopping to chat with you.
2. Sit and be petted by a stranger.
3. Allow a stranger to handle him or her as a groomer or veterinarian would.
4. Walk nicely on a loose lead.
5. Walk calmly through a crowd.
6. Sit and down on command, then stay in a sit or down position while you walk away.
7. Come when called.
8. Casually greet another dog.
9. React confidently to distractions.
10. Accept being left alone with someone other than you and not become overly agitated or nervous.

Schools and Dogs

Schools are getting involved with pet ownership on an educational level. It has been proven that children who are kind to animals are humane in their attitude toward other people as adults.

A dog is a child's best friend, and so children are often primary pet owners, if not the primary caregivers. Unfortunately, they are also the ones most often bitten by dogs. This occurs due to a lack of understanding that pets, no matter how sweet, cuddly and loving, are still animals. Schools, along with parents, dog clubs, dog fanciers and the AKC, are working to change all that with video programs for children not only in grade school, but in the nursery school and pre-kindergarten age group. Teaching youngsters how to be responsible dog owners is important community work. When your dog has a CGC, volunteer to take part in an educational classroom event put on by your dog club.

Boy Scout Merit Badge

A Merit Badge for Dog Care can be earned by any Boy Scout ages 11 to 18. The requirements are not easy, but amount to a complete course in responsible dog care and general ownership. Here are just a few of the things a Scout must do to earn that badge:

Point out ten parts of the dog using the correct names.

Give a report (signed by parent or guardian) on your care of the dog (feeding, food used, housing, exercising, grooming and bathing), plus what has been done to keep the dog healthy.

Explain the right way to obedience train a dog, and demonstrate three comments.

Several of the requirements have to do with health care, including first aid, handling a hurt dog, and the dangers of home treatment for a serious ailment.

The final requirement is to know the local laws and ordinances involving dogs.

There are similar programs for Girl Scouts and 4-H members.

Local Clubs

Local dog clubs are no longer in existence just to put on a yearly dog show. Today, they are apt to be the hub of the community's involvement with pets. Dog clubs conduct educational forums with big-name speakers, stage demonstrations of canine talent in a busy mall and take dogs of various breeds to schools for class-room discussion.

The quickest way to feel accepted as a member in a club is to volunteer your services! Offer to help with something—anything—and watch your popularity (and your interest) grow.

Therapy Dogs

Once your dog has earned that essential CGC and reliably demonstrates a steady, calm temperament, you could look into what therapy dogs are doing in your area.

Therapy dogs go with their owners to visit patients at hospitals or nursing homes, generally remaining on leash but able to coax a pat from a stiffened hand, a smile from a blank face, a few words from sealed lips or a hug from someone in need of love.

Your dog can make a difference in lots of lives.

Nursing homes cover a wide range of patient care. Some specialize in care of the elderly, some in the treatment of specific illnesses, some in physical therapy. Children's facilities also welcome visits from trained therapy dogs for boosting morale in their pediatric patients. Hospice care for the terminally ill and the at-home care of AIDS patients are other areas where this canine visiting is desperately needed. Therapy dog training comes first.

There is a lot more involved than just taking your nice friendly pooch to someone's bedside. Doing therapy dog work involves your own emotional stability as well as that of your dog. But once you have met all the requirements for this work, making the rounds once a week or once a month with your therapy dog is possibly the most rewarding of all community activities.

Disaster Aid

This community service is definitely not for everyone, partly because it is time-consuming. The initial training is rigorous, and there can be no let-up in the continuing workouts, because members are on call 24 hours a day to go wherever they are needed at a moment's notice. But if you think you would like to be able to assist in a disaster, look into search-and-rescue work. The network of search-and-rescue volunteers is worldwide, and all members of the American Rescue Dog Association (ARDA) who are qualified to do this work are volunteers who train and maintain their own dogs.

Physical Aid

Most people are familiar with Seeing Eye dogs, which serve as blind people's eyes, but not with all the other work that dogs are trained to do to assist the disabled. Dogs are also specially trained to pull wheelchairs, carry school books, pick up dropped objects, open and close doors. Some also are ears for the deaf. All these assistance-trained dogs, by the way, are allowed anywhere "No Pet" signs exist (as are therapy dogs when

Making the rounds with your therapy dog can be very rewarding.

properly identified). Getting started in any of this fascinating work requires a background in dog training and canine behavior, but there are also volunteer jobs ranging from answering the phone to cleaning out kennels to providing a foster home for a puppy. You have only to ask.

part four

Beyond
the
Basics

chapter 12

Recommended Reading

Books

ABOUT HEALTH CARE

Ackerman, Lowell. *Guide to Skin and Haircoat Problems in Dogs.* Loveland, Colo.: Alpine Publications, 1994.

Alderton, David. *The Dog Care Manual.* Hauppauge, N.Y.: Barron's Educational Series, Inc., 1986.

American Kennel Club. *American Kennel Club Dog Care and Training.* New York: Howell Book House, 1991.

Bamberger, Michelle, DVM. *Help! The Quick Guide to First Aid for Your Dog.* New York: Howell Book House, 1995.

Carlson, Delbert, DVM, and James Giffin, MD. *Dog Owner's Home Veterinary Handbook.* New York: Howell Book House, 1992.

DeBitetto, James, DVM, and Sarah Hodgson. *You & Your Puppy.* New York: Howell Book House, 1995.

Humphries, Jim, DVM. *Dr. Jim's Animal Clinic for Dogs.* New York: Howell Book House, 1994.

McGinnis, Terri. *The Well Dog Book.* New York: Random House, 1991.

Pitcairn, Richard and Susan. *Natural Health for Dogs.* Emmaus, Pa.: Rodale Press, 1982.

ABOUT DOG SHOWS

Hall, Lynn. *Dog Showing for Beginners.* New York: Howell Book House, 1994.

Nichols, Virginia Tuck. *How to Show Your Own Dog.* Neptune, N. J.: TFH, 1970.

Vanacore, Connie. *Dog Showing, An Owner's Guide.* New York: Howell Book House, 1990.

ABOUT TRAINING

Ammen, Amy. *Training in No Time*. New York: Howell Book House, 1995.

Baer, Ted. *Communicating With Your Dog*. Hauppauge, N.Y.: Barron's Educational Series, Inc., 1989.

Benjamin, Carol Lea. *Dog Problems*. New York: Howell Book House, 1989.

Benjamin, Carol Lea. *Dog Training for Kids*. New York: Howell Book House, 1988.

Benjamin, Carol Lea. *Mother Knows Best*. New York: Howell Book House, 1985.

Benjamin, Carol Lea. *Surviving Your Dog's Adolescence*. New York: Howell Book House, 1993.

Bohnenkamp, Gwen. *Manners for the Modern Dog*. San Francisco: Perfect Paws, 1990.

Dibra, Bashkim. *Dog Training by Bash*. New York: Dell, 1992.

Dunbar, Ian, PhD, MRCVS. *Dr. Dunbar's Good Little Dog Book*, James & Kenneth Publishers, 2140 Shattuck Ave. #2406, Berkeley, Calif. 94704. (510) 658–8588. Order from the publisher.

Dunbar, Ian, PhD, MRCVS. *How to Teach a New Dog Old Tricks*, James & Kenneth Publishers. Order from the publisher; address above.

Dunbar, Ian, PhD, MRCVS, and Gwen Bohnenkamp. Booklets on *Preventing Aggression; Housetraining; Chewing; Digging; Barking; Socialization; Fearfulness; and Fighting*, James & Kenneth Publishers. Order from the publisher; address above.

Evans, Job Michael. *People, Pooches and Problems*. New York: Howell Book House, 1991.

Kilcommons, Brian and Sarah Wilson. *Good Owners, Great Dogs*. New York: Warner Books, 1992.

McMains, Joel M. *Dog Logic—Companion Obedience*. New York: Howell Book House, 1992.

Rutherford, Clarice and David H. Neil, MRCVS. *How to Raise a Puppy You Can Live With*. Loveland, Colo.: Alpine Publications, 1982.

Volhard, Jack and Melissa Bartlett. *What All Good Dogs Should Know: The Sensible Way to Train*. New York: Howell Book House, 1991.

ABOUT BREEDING

Harris, Beth J. Finder. *Breeding a Litter, The Complete Book of Prenatal and Postnatal Care*. New York: Howell Book House, 1983.

Holst, Phyllis, DVM. *Canine Reproduction*. Loveland, Colo.: Alpine Publications, 1985.

Walkowicz, Chris and Bonnie Wilcox, DVM. *Successful Dog Breeding, The Complete Handbook of Canine Midwifery.* New York: Howell Book House, 1994.

ABOUT ACTIVITIES

American Rescue Dog Association. *Search and Rescue Dogs.* New York: Howell Book House, 1991.

Barwig, Susan and Stewart Hilliard. *Schutzhund.* New York: Howell Book House, 1991.

Beaman, Arthur S. *Lure Coursing.* New York: Howell Book House, 1994.

Daniels, Julie. *Enjoying Dog Agility—From Backyard to Competition.* New York: Doral Publishing, 1990.

Davis, Kathy Diamond. *Therapy Dogs.* New York: Howell Book House, 1992.

Gallup, Davis Anne. *Running With Man's Best Friend.* Loveland, Colo.: Alpine Publications, 1986.

Habgood, Dawn and Robert. *On the Road Again With Man's Best Friend.* New England, Mid-Atlantic, West Coast and Southeast editions. Selective guides to area bed and breakfasts, inns, hotels and resorts that welcome guests and their dogs. New York: Howell Book House, 1995.

Holland, Vergil S. *Herding Dogs.* New York: Howell Book House, 1994.

LaBelle, Charlene G. *Backpacking With Your Dog.* Loveland, Colo.: Alpine Publications, 1993.

Simmons-Moake, Jane. *Agility Training, The Fun Sport for All Dogs.* New York: Howell Book House, 1991.

Spencer, James B. *Hup! Training Flushing Spaniels the American Way.* New York: Howell Book House, 1992.

Spencer, James B. *Point! Training the All-Seasons Birddog.* New York: Howell Book House, 1995.

Tarrant, Bill. *Training the Hunting Retriever.* New York: Howell Book House, 1991.

Volhard, Jack and Wendy. *The Canine Good Citizen.* New York: Howell Book House, 1994.

General Titles

Haggerty, Captain Arthur J. *How to Get Your Pet Into Show Business.* New York: Howell Book House, 1994.

McLennan, Bardi. *Dogs and Kids, Parenting Tips.* New York: Howell Book House, 1993.

Moran, Patti J. *Pet Sitting for Profit, A Complete Manual for Professional Success.* New York: Howell Book House, 1992.

Beyond the
Basics

Scalisi, Danny and Libby Moses. *When Rover Just Won't Do, Over 2,000 Suggestions for Naming Your Dog.* New York: Howell Book House, 1993.

Sife, Wallace, PhD. *The Loss of a Pet.* New York: Howell Book House, 1993.

Wrede, Barbara J. *Civilizing Your Puppy.* Hauppauge, N.Y.: Barron's Educational Series, 1992.

Magazines

The AKC GAZETTE, The Official Journal for the Sport of Purebred Dogs. American Kennel Club, 51 Madison Ave., New York, NY.

Bloodlines Journal. United Kennel Club, 100 E. Kilgore Rd., Kalamazoo, MI.

Dog Fancy. Fancy Publications, 3 Burroughs, Irvine, CA 92718

Dog World. Maclean Hunter Publishing Corp., 29 N. Wacker Dr., Chicago, IL 60606.

Videos

"SIRIUS Puppy Training," by Ian Dunbar, PhD, MRCVS. James & Kenneth Publishers, 2140 Shattuck Ave. #2406, Berkeley, CA 94704. Order from the publisher.

"Training the Companion Dog," from Dr. Dunbar's British TV Series, James & Kenneth Publishers. (See address above).

The American Kennel Club produces videos on every breed of dog, as well as on hunting tests, field trials and other areas of interest to purebred dog owners. For more information, write to AKC/Video Fulfillment, 5580 Centerview Dr., Suite 200, Raleigh, NC 27606.

chapter 13

Resources

Breed Clubs

Every breed recognized by the American Kennel Club has a national (parent) club. National clubs are a great source of information on your breed. You can get the name of the secretary of the club by contacting:

The American Kennel Club
51 Madison Avenue
New York, NY 10010
(212) 696-8200

There are also numerous all-breed, individual breed, obedience, hunting and other special-interest dog clubs across the country. The American Kennel Club can provide you with a geographical list of clubs to find ones in your area. Contact them at the above address.

Registry Organizations

Registry organizations register purebred dogs. The American Kennel Club is the oldest and largest in this country, and currently recognizes over 130 breeds. The United Kennel Club registers some breeds the AKC doesn't (including the American Pit Bull Terrier and the Miniature Fox Terrier) as well as many of the same breeds. The others included here are for your reference; the AKC can provide you with a list of foreign registries.

American Kennel Club
51 Madison Avenue
New York, NY 10010

United Kennel Club (UKC)
100 E. Kilgore Road
Kalamazoo, MI 49001-5598

American Dog Breeders Assn.
P.O. Box 1771
Salt Lake City, UT 84110
(Registers American Pit Bull Terriers)

Canadian Kennel Club
89 Skyway Avenue
Etobicoke, Ontario
Canada M9W 6R4

National Stock Dog Registry
P.O. Box 402
Butler, IN 46721
(Registers working stock dogs)

Orthopedic Foundation for Animals (OFA)
2300 E. Nifong Blvd.
Columbia, MO 65201-3856
(Hip registry)

Activity Clubs

Write to these organizations for information on the activities they sponsor.

American Kennel Club
51 Madison Avenue
New York, NY 10010
(Conformation Shows, Obedience Trials, Field Trials and Hunting Tests, Agility, Canine Good

Citizen, Lure Coursing, Herding, Tracking, Earthdog Tests, Coonhunting.)

United Kennel Club
100 E. Kilgore Road
Kalamazoo, MI 49001-5598
(Conformation Shows, Obedience Trials, Agility, Hunting for Various Breeds, Terrier Trials and more.)

North American Flyball Assn.
1342 Jeff St.
Ypsilanti, MI 48198

International Sled Dog Racing Assn.
P.O. Box 446
Norman, ID 83848-0446

North American Working Dog Assn., Inc.
Southeast Kreisgruppe
P.O. Box 833
Brunswick, GA 31521

Trainers

Association of Pet Dog Trainers
P.O. Box 385
Davis, CA 95617
(800) PET–DOGS

American Dog Trainers' Network
161 West 4th St.
New York, NY 10014
(212) 727–7257

National Association of Dog Obedience Instructors
2286 East Steel Rd.
St. Johns, MI 48879

Associations

American Dog Owners Assn.
1654 Columbia Tpk.
Castleton, NY 12033
(Combats anti-dog legislation)

Delta Society
P.O. Box 1080
Renton, WA 98057-1080
(Promotes the human/animal bond through
pet-assisted therapy and other programs)

Dog Writers Assn. of America (DWAA)
Sally Cooper, Secy.
222 Woodchuck Ln.
Harwinton, CT 06791

National Assn. for Search and Rescue (NASAR)
P.O. Box 3709
Fairfax, VA 22038

Therapy Dogs International
6 Hilltop Road
Mendham, NJ 07945